Nation
of
Cowards

Essays on the Ethics of Gun Control

Jeff Snyder

Accurate Press
St. Louis, Missouri

Nation of Cowards
Essays on the Ethics of Gun Control

©2001 by Jeffrey R. Snyder

ISBN 1-888118-07-5 hardcover $24.95
ISBN 1-888118-08-3 paperback $14.95
Printed in the United States of America

Published by Accurate Press, a division of
Accuprint, Inc.
PO Box 86
Lonedell, MO 63060 U.S.A.
1-800-374-4049

for Elizabeth

So they lived as he wanted them to live and all the time there were a few who disappeared. The rabbits became strange in many ways, different from other rabbits. They knew well enough what was happening. But even to themselves they pretended that all was well, for the food was good, they were protected, they had nothing to fear but the one fear; and that struck here and there, never enough at a time to drive them away. They forgot the ways of wild rabbits. They forgot El-ahrairah, for what use had they for tricks and cunning, living in the enemy's warren and paying his price? They found out other marvelous arts to take the place of tricks and old stories. They danced in ceremonious greetings. They sang songs like the birds and made Shapes on the walls; and though these could help them not at all, yet they passed the time and enabled them to tell themselves that they were splendid fellows, the very flower of Rabbitry. . .

Richard Adams,
Watership Down

TABLE OF CONTENTS

FOREWORD

This book is a collection of essays about what may be loosely described as the ethics of owning, carrying and using arms, and of the efforts to restrict those activities. The essays are not, for the most part, about whether gun control *works*, that is, does or does not succeed in reducing crime, preventing accidents and suicides, ennoble a society's inhabitants or create a more peaceful, civil society. Nor, correspondingly, do the essays argue that the individual right to keep and bear arms *works*, that is, succeeds in empowering a meaningful number of citizens to preserve life, limb or property, reduces violent crime, or serves as a deterrent to genocide or governmental tyranny, and thereby creates a more peaceful, civil society. All of these claims have been made and argued by others in numerous books, essays, op-ed pieces and criminological studies; they are the regular fodder of the gun control debate.

For the most part, I am not here engaged in the business of recommending, justifying, or critiquing policy prescriptions on the basis of the promised or probable benefits, a process I find extremely questionable on both epistemological and ethical grounds. Here the reader will not find statistical chapter and verse quoted at him, or summaries and methodological critiques of criminological studies and data sets, all working toward a grand conclusion about the factual truth of gun control. Those looking for factual vindication of their cherished opinions on the subject are better served to look elsewhere.

Instead, the essays generally endeavor to uncover and bring into stark relief the quite different values and choices that underlie gun control and the liberty to keep and bear arms. It is not factual knowledge about the results of law or policy that these essays seek but knowledge about our character. Thus, the essays are not fundamentally about guns at all. They are, foremost, about the way we see ourselves, the kind of people we intend to be, the attitudes or beliefs that underlie the impulse to control firearms, and the ethical or political consequences of decisions founded in those attitudes or beliefs.

Essays have been grouped by dominant, related themes. Those under the heading, "Bearing Arms," focus predominantly on the values or ethics underlying a personal resolve to resist crime, or to undertake the responsibility and develop the wherewithal to defend oneself from violence. The essays examine — and criticize — common arguments that the employment of lethal violence in self-defense is best left exclusively to the state.

The essays grouped under "Against Prevention" endeavor to uncover and examine the ethical assumptions and consequences inherent in gun control legislation. Gun control laws generally proscribe innocent conduct in order to *prevent* crime, that is, they criminalize a harmless activity by A, such as selling a gun or carrying a gun into a post office or within a "school zone," not because the proscribed act in itself harms anyone, but because it is a step or means to the commission of a real crime, like murder or assault. A's innocent conduct is thus both controlled and criminalized in order to prevent the subsequent, truly criminal conduct of either A or B.

In this, gun control is only one example of the far more general and prevalent use of law as an instrument of prevention. The nation's "War on Drugs," banking and securities laws, etc. are rich sources of other examples of such laws. For example, bankers are required to report transactions involving more than $10,000 — in part to aid in tracing money laundering from drug sales. Thus, every American's financial affairs become the Drug Enforcement Agency's business, and bankers face risk of criminal prosecution for paperwork, in order to provide the DEA a tool of enforcing *other* laws against a handful of actual drug criminals.

Unless debated on Second Amendment grounds, discussions of gun control measures are generally limited to questioning the efficacy of this type of restriction, i.e., whether controlling A's conduct may be reasonably expected to succeed in preventing either A's or B's crime. Or such measures may be attacked on cost-benefit grounds — that the expected benefits are grossly disproportionate to the costs involved in making the measures work, and are therefore a waste of limited resources better spent elsewhere on a more achievable goal. Or, they are attacked on grounds of inconsistency or irrationality in prioritizing.[1]

The essays under "Against Prevention" take a different tack, drawing out the implications of the use of law as a tool of prevention, and endeavoring to show its destructive, self-contradictory nature. By criminalizing inherently innocent conduct, such laws, it is argued, *necessarily* ignore or eliminate the moral foundation of law, thereby destroying their own claim to respect. Law so used then becomes nothing more than an instrument of brute force. Since prevention efforts are necessarily targeted at conduct that is not itself immoral or criminal but which *precedes* criminality, law as

---

1 For example, in response to the claim that guns should be restricted or eliminated because *x* number of children are killed each year in gun accidents, a gun rights advocate may point out, correctly, that 3*x* children drown in swimming pools each year, and ask why the gun control advocate is not advocating banning swimming pools or laws that limit swimming to adults. This response works on at least two levels. Taken literally, it suggests irrationality or inconsistency in the gun control advocate. If saving children's lives is the goal, why are you not focusing your efforts first on graver dangers? That is, it challenges the advocate with irrationality in prioritizing. This is only a surface attack, however. More fundamentally, it calls into question the sincerity with which the gun control advocate in fact wants to ban guns in order to save lives, and raises the question whether saving children's lives is merely a rhetorical justification and the real reason that the control proponent wants to ban guns lies elsewhere.

an instrument of brute force is applied, intentionally, to the law-abiding themselves, *a fact which will eventually become apparent to them.*

Generally, the explicit or implicit moral criterion for evaluating gun control is social utilitarianism, i.e., the greatest good for the greatest number, where the greatest good is taken, self-evidently, as lives saved, harm or injury averted, and dollars saved (e.g., reduced medical care costs from a decrease in gun shot wounds). *Generally, both gun control proponents and opponents labor, and seek justification, under the same criterion* — the supporters of control arguing that more lives will be saved by restricting or banning guns and the proponents of the right to keep and bear arms arguing that more lives will be lost and greater harm will result if people are rendered defenseless. Hence the teeming criminological research to establish just what the true facts are, and intense debate over the validity of those studies and their findings.

The essays grouped under the heading, "Against Utility," question the use of the utilitarian ethic on a number of levels, for example, whether mere preservation of life or avoidance of harm is in fact a "greatest good" (a theme that runs through various other essays in this book), and whether the utilitarian justification proclaimed by gun control advocates is merely espoused or actually believed. Most significantly, however, the essays endeavor to demonstrate that utilitarianism, as a results-driven ethic, is incompatible with a theory that individuals have certain fundamental rights (whether that be a right to life, a right to keep and bear arms, free speech, due process or otherwise). Efforts are also made to demonstrate that the utilitarian ethic espoused by gun control proponents freely sanctions sacrificing the lives of some to save the lives of others. Yes, this ethic "cares" about people — but only *en masse*; it loves humanity — as a lump sum. Particular individuals simply don't count. A is deprived of the means to defend himself from violent crime so that B, a child, will not accidentally shoot himself, C, a distraught teenager, will not commit suicide, and D, a criminal, will not be able to hold up a convenience store. The essence of this ethic, quite simply, is the belief that civilization depends on (involuntary) human sacrifice.

The overwhelming weight of modern historical and legal scholarship establishes that the Second Amendment secures a right of individuals to keep and bear arms suitable for self-defense and service in a militia, and the essays in this book take this as established fact.[2] The essays under the heading, *"Second Amendment,"* then, do not argue the amendment's meaning, or criticize the state's right interpretation of the amendment. One simply proclaims that the emperor has no clothes, and makes a case for the obvious —— that the amendment is no longer respected and has no force, politically or legally. Gun owners are a minority (albeit a fairly large one) reduced to special interest group politics in order to preserve the remaining liberty to keep and bear arms.

In *Marbury v. Madison* (1803), the Supreme Court announced that its role in our constitutional government was "to say what the law is." The second essay in this group, "The Unbearable Lightness of Rights," questions the Supreme Court's authority to define and interpret our individual rights (and by implication, to create new ones), and argues that the Court's opinions regarding

---

2 As summarized by historian Joyce Lee Malcolm,
"The Second Amendment was meant to accomplish two distinct goals, each perceived as crucial to the maintenance of liberty. First, it was meant to guarantee the individual's right to have arms for self-defense and self-preservation. Such an individual right was a legacy of the English bill of rights. This is also plain from American colonial practice, the debates over the constitution, and state proposals for what was to become the Second Amendment. . . . The second and related objective concerned the militia, and it is the coupling of these two objectives that has caused the most confusion. The customary American militia necessitated an armed public, and Madison's original version of the amendment, as well as those suggested by the states, describe the militia as either 'composed of' or 'including' the body of the people. A select militia was regarded as little better than a standing army."

To Keep and Bear Arms — The Origins of an Anglo-American Right, Cambridge Mass.: Harvard University Press, 1994, pp. 162-63. For scholarly legal investigations of the meaning of the Second Amendment, see, for example, Don B. Kates, "Handgun Prohibition and the Original Meaning of the Second Amendment," 82 *Michigan Law Review* 204 (1983); Sanford Levinson, "The Embarrassing Second Amendment," 99 *Yale Law Journal* 637 (1989); William Van Alstyne, "The Second Amendment and the Personal Right to Arms," 43 *Duke Law Journal* 1236 (1994). A collection of citations to other articles on the Second Amendment can be found in Glenn Harlan Reynolds, "A Critical Guide to the Second Amendment," 62 *Tennessee Law Review* 465 (1995), n. 18.

individual rights are not binding either on the people or the other branches of the federal government. A reader must be careful here, for I do not claim that the Court may not express an opinion on the meaning of our rights, or an opinion on whether a law exceeds constitutional bounds. I state only that its opinions, insofar as they concern our rights, are not binding and cannot have the force of law. The Court's power to expound our rights is limited to its power to persuade.

Recognizing that many will have serious doubts concerning this line of argument (as it is contrary to virtually the entire history and practice of Supreme Court review and supposed binding nature of Court opinions on hallowed subjects), the article continues by questioning the legitimacy of the philosophy of rights embodied in current court opinions, in which rights are simply weighty interests subject to a balancing test and may be outweighed by, and must yield to, a "compelling state interest." In the Court's rights jurisprudence, in other words, the state (i.e., government at all levels), is the "heavy," for the Court accords final and greatest weight to the state. Only the state's interests are ever "compelling."

This article, which was written years after "The Second Amendment is Dead," reflects a very different view of the Supreme Court's role in our constitutional system than was tacitly assumed in "Dead," and I apologize if the dissonance is disconcerting. However, the two articles, taken together, clearly stake out a single trajectory of thought on the question of where ultimate responsibility for the preservation of our rights lies.

The final essay in this group, "Walter Mitty's Second Amendment," adopts a childish mechanism — the form of a fairy tale — to illustrate the fallacies inherent in an instrumentalist view of individual rights. The story imagines a fair land where the citizens retain, in full measure, their right to keep and bear arms, but have been reduced to slaves in all other respects. At its simplest level, the story is about the idiocy of being a one-issue citizen. More fundamentally, the story is about the irrelevance and inconsequence of rights in the hands of a debased people. Most fundamentally of all, the story illustrates that the mere existence of, and respect for, rights does not vouchsafe particular or necessarily "good" results. It is, again, people's character that is fundamental.

While gun control advocates seem to neither notice nor care, their proposals, when enacted into law, are radicalizing an ever-growing number of gun owners. This is not merely because of the contempt or disdain gun control laws express for a way of life that tens of millions of Americans have long associated with the ownership and use of firearms. Nor is it merely due to the fact that, by designing laws that are targeted specifically at law-abiding gun owners, the laws implicitly blame and punish them for the problem of gun violence. More fundamentally, gun control laws radicalize gun owners because they are enacted in blatant disregard of the Second Amendment. From this, from the rationalizations explaining why the amendment does not really mean what it plainly says, and the refusal by the Supreme Court to even hear a Second Amendment case and declare its meaning since 1939 (*U.S. v. Miller*), it is obvious that our lawmakers, president and courts have either no or, what amounts to the same thing, only selective respect for our supposed founding document and supreme law. That is, it is at once apparent that they will recognize it when it suits their purpose, and otherwise not. With each additional gun control law, then, it becomes more and more apparent that our legislators, president and courts are fundamentally lawless, recognizing no authority higher than their own preferences and mere majority rule or, in the case of the courts, the personal beliefs of the judges. Laws enacted in such blatant disregard of a fundamental right make manifest the fact that politics is a confidence game in which the legislators and the courts capitalize upon and trade off of the people's respect for the nation's supreme law to establish legitimacy for their laws and rulings, a veneration and respect they themselves do not share. Gun control is thus providing the occasion for, and disposing larger numbers of people to, recognizing the destruction of individual rights and the illegitimacy of the federal government. When this line has been crossed, it is not easily re-established.

The enactment of the Brady Bill in 1993 and assault-weapon ban in 1994 were watershed moments in this regard. My editor at *American Handgunner,* Cameron Hopkins, received a number of letters questioning when it was appropriate for a people, seeing a steady stream of incremental encroachments upon their fundamental rights, to take up arms against their government. One letter warned that we could not wait too long, lest we be like the frog in the pot, who never jumps out and is cooked because the heat is raised gradually. Cameron asked me to address this issue in an essay called "The Line in the Sand." The essay contains some reflections on revolution, and on how we might restore self-government. It was an assignment I undertook with some trepidation. Not having previously given much thought to the subject, I feared what conclusions I would reach. The answer proved surprising — to me at least. The loss of rights is in every case preceded by a rejection of personal responsibility (in the case of the Second Amendment, the responsibility to defend oneself and one's community or nation), and shifting of that responsibility to unaccountable and nameless others (government). Liberty can be preserved only by retaining responsibility. To reclaim rights and liberty, we must begin by reclaiming responsibility.

INTRODUCTION

Guns and the Instrumental Theory of Salvation

G un control is generally offered as a means of preventing suicide and accidental death, and of reducing violent crime, or at least reducing the amount of harm caused by violent crime. It is generally justified, then, by the results it promises: saving lives, increasing public safety. Its logic and appeal are simple and powerful: eliminate or restrict access to guns, and we limit our ability to hurt ourselves, and one another.

In promising an environmental solution to a behavioral problem, however, it leaves the behavioral problem untouched. The underlying criminal desire, the dark impulse, flash of anger, recklessness, even simple negligence will remain, unaltered, unabated, but the mortal instrument with which to "act out" these states of mind will be absent, out of reach. The essential modus operandi of gun control, then, is to render certain dangerous states of mind impotent, or to re-direct them so that they act or "express" themselves in a less lethal fashion, by controlling access to a deadly instrument. In this manner gun control embodies or rests upon what we may call an instrumental theory of salvation.

The right to keep and bear arms is generally justified as a necessary corollary of the right of self-defense and of the principle of government by consent. If the individual has a right to protect his life from criminal violence threatening death or grievous bodily harm, he of necessity must have the right to tools fitted to that purpose,[1] else the "right" is merely nominal, a cruel hoax. If government rules only by the consent of the people, then the people must have a right to possess and wield the means of resistance against the day that government oversteps its bounds. A "principal" who had no final recourse or means of protecting himself against the *ultra vires* acts of his nominal "agent," or of resisting an agent who sought to enslave him, would in no sense be a "principal."

At a debate over gun control at the Cato Institute in 1997, my opponent, a member of the Center to Prevent Handgun Violence, went so far as to deny the existence of a right of self-defense. This is certainly going back to first principles to establish a position for gun control, and is noteworthy because few representatives of gun control organizations are willing to go so far. Selling gun control to the public by telling people that they have no right to defend their lives or those of their loved ones from violent criminal assault poses obvious "marketing" and "public relations" difficulties. It is far more common to hear claims that guns are not really all that effective for self-defense, or that they are far more likely to harm the owner or his loved ones than a criminal. That is, the arguments do not make a frontal assault on the legitimacy of self-defense; they simply assert that the probabilities are that it won't pay to exercise that right, or that the opportunities to exercise that right are illusory.

My opponent was certainly correct, in the sense that this right is nowhere created or granted in the statute books, case law or in the U.S. Constitution. Unfortunately, gun control proponents who go so far appear to have no appreciation for the difficulties they are creating by denying the existence of this natural right. A fair case may be made that, more than any other right, the right to keep and bear arms implicates the entire theory by which modern govern-

---

1 By "fitted to that purpose," I intend to exclude, of course, weapons whose indiscriminate or overly powerful nature renders them particularly unsuitable for purely individual self-defense, such as land mines, grenades, tanks, mortar, stinger missiles, F-16s, and nuclear bombs.

ments are legitimated. Social contract theorists like Hobbes and consent theorists like Locke derive the legitimacy of government by starting with the natural rights of each *individual*, among the principal of which is the right of self-defense. If individuals have no natural right of self-defense that (at least logically) precedes government, it is difficult, if not impossible, to construct a theory by which "the people" are the source of governmental authority, and the coercive power of government is legitimated by consent.

Consent is neither real nor meaningful unless born of a power and right to both say no and to act on the basis of no. Denial of a natural right of self-defense thus entails no less than the destruction of the very foundation of consent. It is no answer to this to argue that consent is sufficiently secured by the power to vote, so that, once government is formed, people need no longer have recourse to violent means of enforcing a "no." That could be true only if it were impossible for majorities to act tyrannically or, to state it positively, only if anything majorities decided to do was, *ipso facto*, legitimate and rightly forced upon others. This, however, is readily recognized as an ethic generally summed up in the phrase, "might makes right," or "the law of the jungle."[2]

---

2 Suppose that two men and a woman who have previously formed a mutual assistance society for various social and economic purposes are, upon motion duly made and seconded by the two men in complete accordance with Roberts Rules of Order, to vote on the decision whether the woman must have sex with the men. Assume that the corporate charter and by-laws creating this society fail to make any specific mention of the woman's "natural" rights. Imagine endeavoring to seriously maintain, now, that the outcome of the vote will be binding on the woman simply because she is entitled to have her views on the subject duly represented, i.e., to debate the merits of the proposal with the other members of the society prior to the vote, and to then vote on the proposal. Imagine, that is, maintaining that even though she votes "no," if the measure passes she will be *presumed* to have consented to sex with the men and that it will therefore *not* be rape because of her *previous* consent to the formation of the society and its ground rules and because she has the additional right to continue petitioning the other members of her society to repeal the law. Suppose that the vote is taken, again in full compliance with Roberts Rules of Order, and the proposal passes. Try, now, to seriously maintain that because she was outvoted, she *must* submit. Defend, now, the proposition that if she believes that this new law is beyond the authority granted to the society in its founding documents, she may contest its legitimacy in the courts, but in the mean time she must submit. In sum, imagine trying to seriously argue in this situation that she may say no, but she may not act on the basis of a no by resisting her rape *immediately* and to the utmost. This perhaps will give you some sense of both the logical and practical necessity of a right to keep and bear arms in a democratic government by consent.

3

It fairly follows that to deny an individual right to keep and bear arms, that is, a right to possess the means with which to enforce (or at least act upon) a "no," is also to simultaneously affirm that government is *not* founded upon consent, and is thus not legitimated by consent. Or stated otherwise, if we are to deny a right to keep and bear arms but maintain that our government is founded upon consent, the theory of government by consent is then simply a fiction employed to hide and legitimate the exercise of raw power, an updated version of Plato's Foundation Myth.[3]

While strong principled justifications thus exist for a right to keep and bear arms, the right is also sometimes justified by reference to its promised benefits. Claimants or supporters of the right generally do not stop in maintaining that guns are tools that are eminently useful for self-defense; they often go further, and argue

---

3 Plato has Socrates speaking about forming the perfect state:

'Now I wonder if we could contrive one of those convenient stories we were talking about a few minutes ago,' I asked, 'some magnificent myth that would in itself carry conviction to our whole community, including, if possible, the Guardians themselves?'

. . . I shall try to persuade first the Rulers and Soldiers, and then the rest of the community, that the upbringing and education we have given them was all something that happened to them only in a dream. In reality they were fashioned and reared, and their arms and equipment manufactured, in the depths of the earth, and Earth herself, their mother, brought them up, when they were complete, into the light of day; so now they must think of the land in which they live as their mother and protect her if she is attacked, while their fellow-citizens they must regard as brothers born of the same mother earth.'

. . . 'We shall,' I said, 'tell our citizens the following tale:

"You are, all of you in this community, brothers. But when god fashioned you, he added gold in the composition of those of you who are qualified to be rulers (which is why their prestige is greatest); he put silver in the Auxiliaries, and iron and bronze in the farmers and other workers. Now since you are all of the same stock, though your children will commonly resemble their parents, occasionally a silver child will be born of golden parents, or a golden child of silver parents, and so on. Therefore the first and most important of god's commandments to the Rulers is that in the exercise of their function as guardians their principal care must be to watch the mixture of metals in the characters their children. If one of their own children has traces of bronze or iron in its makeup, they must harden their hearts, assign in its proper value, and degrade it to the ranks of the industrial and agricultural class where it properly belongs; similarly, if a child of this class is born with gold or silver in its nature, they will promote it appropriately to be a Guardian or Auxiliary. And this they must do because there is a prophecy that the State will be ruined when it has Guardians of silver or bronze." This is the story. Do you know of any way of making them believe it?' 'Not in the first generation,' he said, 'but you might succeed with the second and later generations.' 'Even so it should serve to increase their loyalty to the state and to each other. For I think I understand what you mean.'

— Plato, The Republic, Book III, 414b - 415, Penguin Books, Second Edition, 1974, translated by Desmond Lee.

that permitting the carry of arms will reduce the amount of violent crime in society. Neither do they generally stop at maintaining that firearms are tools that are eminently useful for resisting tyranny; they often go further, and argue that the widespread possession of arms deters the worst government excesses, such as massive or rampant violation of civil liberties, a military coup d' é- tat, or genocide, because of the risk of armed uprising, civil war or revolution itself. In short, they, too, claim that both individuals and society will realize various benefits by controlling access to a deadly weapon — in this case, by insuring that the law permits nearly all competent law-abiding citizens to own and carry weapons. In this respect, they, too, evince an instrumentalist view of salvation, and differ from their opponents principally in their assessment of which means, prohibition or liberty, produces the greater benefits.

In both cases, the characteristic means of argument, which we may dub "instrumentalism," and which selects as its focal point the existence or availability of mere instruments, effectively assigns causal agency to guns, attributing to them a power to create good or evil. But guns are not protagonists in the human drama; they have no will, no personhood. Not being moral agents, they are not *responsible* for consequences. If guns do not kill people (as gun owners like to say), neither do they deter crime nor serve as a bulwark against tyranny. If people kill people, then only people resist crime and fight tyranny. *In every case it is the individual's character, intention and resolve that is fundamental.* In every case, the action rests on a prior decision or resolve to act — that way. *These decisions are not givens.*

To speak about the gun as though it were a protagonist in the human drama is not merely to adopt a literary device to structure a particular kind of dramatic narrative, nor to select a focal point that renders the quantitative measurement and analysis of multifaceted behavioral phenomena possible. It is to both ignore and obscure the reality that character and individual choice are responsible for the results. Instrumentalism, whether believed or used merely as a narrative device, ignores human agency. Worse, it effectively presumes that the existing, underlying behaviors generating the results under consideration may be taken either as givens, or fixed, such that the results may be expressed simply as a function of the existence or non-existence of a tool. The gun becomes a determinant of human action; we become functionaries of the gun.

An example will help clarify this. Let's take a look at what is perhaps the most famous anti-gun statistic of all time. In 1986, Dr. Arthur Kellerman and Donald Reay published a report in the New England Journal of Medicine in which they concluded that a gun in the home is 43 times more likely to be used for a suicide, accidental gunshot death or a criminal homicide than to kill a criminal intruder in self-defense.[4] The meaning and usefulness of this statistic are extremely questionable,[5] but for our purposes we may simply take the reported finding at face value.

Note that the very form of the finding attributes determinant status to firearms, as if it were the presence of firearms that effected this result. The persons involved are simply not mentioned at all; the actions or behaviors leading to events which befall them (homicides in their homes) are simply abstracted out, represented as a simple function of the presence of "a gun in the home." The gun has acquired causal agency, its presence has been rendered akin to a force of nature. And man's character and freedom have vanished, as irrelevant!

As a statistical finding, the reported conclusion summarizes a factual relationship among events that have occurred. The presumed purpose of uncovering or generating such information,

---

4 314 New England Journal of Medicine 1557 - 1560 (1986).

5 One problem is that 86 percent of the gunshot victims were suicides and not victims of accidents or domestic quarrels, and it is very difficult, if not impossible, to determine accurately how many suicides would not have occurred but for the presence of a gun. While, theoretically, the availability of the gun makes it possible to commit an "impulsive" suicide that would not occur if the suicidal person had to make a greater or more prolonged effort, several countries with very strict gun control, such as Japan, have higher suicide rates than the United States. If one excludes suicides, the "43 times" statistic becomes a far less imposing "6 times" statistic, and even that number is seriously misleading as a supposed measure of the lack of utility of firearms in the home. For a criticism of this study, see Daniel D. Polsby, "Firearms and Crime: Report to the [Kansas] Governor's Task Force on Crime," Independent Institute of Oakland, California, 1997.

however, is to provide a meaningful basis for *future* action. But by relying on information cast in an instrumentalist form for purposes of deciding a *future* course of conduct, whether by individual initiative or policy prescription, we effectively transform a mere statement of fact into a Law of Human Nature Regarding Firearm Use through the aid, additionally, of the unstated assumption that the past provides a reliable indication of the future: this is what has happened, and *this is what will continue to happen*, unless we "do something."[6]

And what does "doing something" entail? Because human agency, freedom and choice have been ignored in the form of the finding, they are likewise ignored in the proposed solution. Since the results were expressed as a function of the presence of a mere instrument at a particular location to begin with, the solution is equally instrumentalist, namely, to ban firearm possession in the home. Since causal agency has been assigned to the gun, the only way to change the result is to eliminate the gun; since the presence

---

6 The Securities Exchange Commission, ever watchful that investors not be misled by glowing financial histories, requires companies to warn that "past performance is no guaranty of future results" in their prospectuses, offering memoranda and even advertising brochures. Alas! No such warning accompanies the findings of social scientists, who seem quite content to let the consumers of their products treat their findings as though they had uncovered invariable laws of human nature! How then do the findings change over time or differ from state to state or country to country? How is it that an analysis of the same factors at another time or location will not, or cannot be guaranteed to generate the same results? The criminologist would answer that other factors come into play, other factors that we have failed to identify, or which may not be quantifiable; other factors become significant, while some of the initial factors may cease to be statistically significant. Yes, but it is precisely the fact of change, that the statistical analysis cannot eliminate, account for or predict, that is the heart of the matter. The elements of the set that have statistical significance at any given point in time cannot account for the permutation of the set. The universe of potential significant factors is not a closed set, so it is manifest error to attribute determinant status to any known element, or any group of known elements of the set, and fundamentally indeterminate how much we may count on controlling the result by controlling or manipulating the known elements in the set. In ethical rather than mathematical language this is expressed thus: *we* are the agents, and we are *free*. Now if the findings are not invariable, how may they serve as a reliable guide to future action? If changeable, how may we know when to cease relying on them? Evidently only *after the fact*, when a new analysis discloses that the previous results no longer obtain; then we may adjust our future behavior to adhere to revelations about the more recent past, and so on *ad infinitum* — a process that bears a striking resemblance to a dog chasing its tail. If the results are reliable only for the foreseeable future on the basis of the assumption that past performance is a pretty good guaranty of future results (the SEC's opinion notwithstanding), how may they serve as a basis for enacting laws that will be on the statute books for decades if not centuries, binding future generations not yet born?

of the gun controls the behavior, the only way to change the behavior is to eliminate the gun. Whether or not, however, we eliminate the gun, we have become functionaries of the gun. Even *when* we eliminate it and thereby "save" ourselves, we eliminate it *because* we are functionaries of the gun.

Now we arrive at the critical paradox of instrumentalism. In its gun control variation, its end point is to pass a law eliminating, or restricting access to the gun; that way lies salvation. But the act of passing and complying with a law, and the very notion of law itself, assumes that men are *free*, that is, have the capacity to conform their behavior to a self-given rule of conduct. Instrumentalism thus leads *always* to the contradiction that men whose conduct is supposed determined by the power exercised by external factors (in this case the presence of the gun), and so who are not free and therefore cannot be responsible for the events which befall them (in this case, experiencing a homicide in the home), propose to exercise a freedom they supposedly do not have by legislating to themselves a rule that, if adhered to (that is, by exercising a capacity for responsibility they supposedly do not have), will free them from consequences just posited as beyond their control.[7]

But if we have the capacity to free ourselves from the undesirable consequences of keeping a gun in the home by adherence to one law of conduct (banning guns in the home), why can't we free ourselves from those consequences by adherence to a different rule of conduct that would accomplish the same results — adherence to laws against suicide and homicide? Or take another example. If

---

7 It is often a consequence of our passionate attachment to our beliefs that we are capable of seeing the contradictions or flaws in our opponents' positions, without realizing that our own positions may embody the same errors. Although I have used an example of gun control instrumentalism, a parallel example can be constructed for gun rights instrumentalism, which would lead to the obverse of the same paradox or contradiction. In that case, the right to keep and bear arms would be supposed to create the positive benefits that gun rights advocates argue are associated with gun ownership: lower crime rates, and deterrence or prevention of governmental tyranny. We then have the spectacle of people who are said to be "free," for example, from governmental tyranny or from violent crime, enjoying that status because it has been *determined* or produced by the existence and power of an object. Thus, people are, again, simultaneously described as both free and functionaries of the gun. The ridiculousness of such a position is illustrated in the essay, "Walter Mitty's Second Amendment."

people cannot be trusted to responsibly carry handguns outside the home for self-protection, why is the answer to prohibit the activity? Again, if people have the capacity to conform their behavior to a rule of conduct, necessarily presumed in the passage of a law prohibiting the carry of arms, why is the answer not an alternative rule that requires them to obtain a specified type of training that would render them fit for the task? Evidently, it is because the former course does not ask all that much of us, and the latter demands too much, or that we don't trust ourselves to be able to live up to the demands of the latter.

The choice of the "solution" is, therefore, highly revealing of what we believe about ourselves. And the choice habitually made by gun control proponents reveals that they have the most dismal assessment of our capabilities; safety inheres, as with little children, in keeping us away from sharp or dangerous objects.[8] Here we see, then, that instrumentalism is a way of writing off our ethical capacity — no, by blinding us to our own agency, is the very *creation* of diminished capacity.[9]

There is an explanation for instrumentalism's contradictory double-mindedness, this tacit need for freedom and responsibility in the midst of claims that our behaviors or their consequences are dictated by object or circumstance. It arises because people wish so very desperately to be *not* responsible, and so dream of worlds which work without their participation, filled with wondrous mechanisms that shoulder for them the terrible burdens — of living. That is a topic, however, for another day. More important for our purposes is that the contradiction inherent in instrumentalism

---

8 It might be argued, in criticism of this view, that gun control laws seek only to keep guns out of the "wrong" hands, and not everyone's, and that the statements just made are therefore too sweeping. Such a criticism, however, is belied by the fact that numerous gun laws, such as the assault weapon ban, apply across the board, and others, like the Brady Act, begin with a universal presumption of incapacity (a fact discussed in greater detail in some of the essays). Equally significant, the criticism is belied by the fact that the announced or implicit goal of many gun control activists is complete prohibition, with the possible exception, in some cases, of ownership and use solely for "sporting purposes" under tightly guarded conditions. For example, it is not unusual for gun control activists to claim, when a particular measure is passed, that it is "a good *first* step."

9 Although I focus here on gun control instrumentalism, I emphasize that the arguments and statements are identically true for gun rights instrumentalism.

demonstrates that instrumentalism is a lie, for it cannot get by without secretly importing, as *deus ex machina*, that which it originally denies — human agency, with its twin pillars of freedom and responsibility.

The gun is only a tool. Its use depends entirely on the character and purpose of the one who wields it. Like other tools, it increases the efficacy and magnifies the result of action and intention. With a gun, a 100 pound woman can successfully defend her life from a vicious assault by a 170-pound man. On the other hand, if she is careless or foolhardy, the gun will more readily manifest and magnify the result of that behavior. Being more effective, it is less forgiving of error, impulse, mindlessness. Yet in one case and the other, the gun has not done good, the gun has not done evil. As a tool, it *enables* a man or woman to do greater good or greater evil. Take it away, and you have reduced man's capacity to do harm, yes, but you have also reduced man's capacity to do good. That we entertain serious discussions about eliminating guns speaks not so much to the "evil" nature of the thing itself — it has no moral nature — or to our revulsion over the harm wrought with it, as it does about our beliefs in our own capacity and willingness to do good, to undertake those actions in service of the good that would require or recommend the use of that tool. We see no good in guns because we have drawn a line through performing those good deeds for which a gun would be necessary or advisable and, what is more chilling, doubt our own capacity to do so. For this reason more than any other, there is no salvation through gun control.

Endnote: unconditional non-violence

The attentive reader will have noticed that while I described justifications for the right to keep and bear arms both on principle and by reference to promised results, I described a justification for gun control only by reference to its promised results. This is not because a principled justification for gun control does not exist; quite the contrary. One does, and it is decisive. The principle is founded on Christ's injunctions, in the Sermon on the Mount, to "resist not evil," to "turn the other cheek," and to "love one's enemies" (Matthew 5 : 38 - 48). On this basis, it is immoral or sinful to use violence to resist evil. Violence against our fellow man is never permissible and never proper, not even in self-defense. He who endeavors to live a Christian life, then, does not bear arms against another.

I hasten to add two caveats. First, it does not follow from an injunction to not resist evil with violence that you are obliged to cooperate with it. Clearly, you are bound to act on the basis of God's law and upon conscience, even if this means being imprisoned or even losing your life because, for example, the government seeks to compel you to serve in a war to kill others or because the Nazis will kill you unless you disclose the location of the Jews that you have helped to hide. Second, for anyone who considers himself or herself to be an atheist or agnostic, it does not answer the claim that all violence is immoral or sinful to argue or believe that Christ was not really God, or even that God does not exist. Christ has made a claim about the way it is proper for man to live. Denying His divinity does not answer or even begin to address the claim.

The essays in this book do not come to terms with this principle of complete non-violence, and that is a grave weakness. It is omitted from discussion, though, not because it is not worth considering, but because the same principle that prohibits the use of arms for self-defense condemns their use, and the use of all force, to impose rules of conduct upon others. Christ's injunction contains no sanitizing exception for the use of force or violence by government, and equally condemns the coercive machinery of the state: laws, police, courts and prisons. In short, I omit an extended discussion of the principle in this Introduction because, while the principle that it is wrong to resist evil with violence does indeed imply that individuals should not use guns against their fellow man, it likewise denies validity to a legal regime of gun control, and thus does not support that cause. People may endeavor to *persuade* their fellow citizens that they should not own, carry or use firearms, but they may not *compel* them to act on that basis. For a thorough, consistent and impassioned exposition of the radical implications of Christ's teachings in this regard, I strongly recommend *The Law of Violence and The Law of Love*, by Leo Tolstoy (1908).

BEARING ARMS

"A man's character is his destiny."

Heraclitus

A Nation of Cowards

Our society has reached a pinnacle of self-expression and respect for individuality rare or unmatched in the history of civilization. Our entire popular culture — from fashion magazines to the cinema — positively screams the matchless worth of the individual, glories in eccentricity, nonconformity, independent judgment, and self-determination. This enthusiasm is reflected in the prevalent notion that helping someone entails increasing that person's "self-esteem"; that if a person properly values himself, he will naturally be a happy, productive and, in some inexplicable fashion, responsible member of society.

And yet, while people are encouraged to revel in their individuality and incalculable self-worth, the media and the law enforcement establishment continually advise us that, when confronted with the threat of lethal violence, we should not resist, but simply give the attacker what he wants. If the crime under consideration is rape, there is some notable waffling on this point, and the discussion quickly moves to how the woman can change her behavior to avoid or minimize the risk of rape, and the various ridiculous, non-lethal weapons she may acceptably carry, such as whistles, keys, mace, or that weapon which really sends shivers down a rapist's spine, the portable cellular phone.

Now how can this be? How can a person who values himself so highly calmly accept the indignity of a criminal assault? How can one who believes that the essence of his dignity lies in his self-determination passively accept the forceful deprivation of that self-determination? How can he, quietly, with great dignity and poise, simply hand over the goods?

The assumption, of course, is that there is no inconsistency. The advice to not resist a criminal assault and simply hand over the goods is founded on the notion that one's life is of incalculable value, and that no amount of property is worth it. Put aside, for the moment, the outrageousness of the suggestion that a criminal who proffers lethal violence should be treated as if he has institut-ed a new social contract: "I will not hurt or kill you if you give me what I want." For years, feminists have labored to educate people that rape is not about sex, but about domination, degradation, and control. Evidently, someone needs to inform the law enforcement establishment and the media that kidnapping, robbery, carjacking and assault are not about property.

Crime is not only a complete disavowal of the social contract, but also a commandeering of the intended victim's person and lib-erty. If the individual's dignity lies in the fact that he is a moral agent engaging in actions of his own will, in free exchange with others, then crime always violates the victim's dignity. It is, in fact, an act of enslavement. Your wallet, your purse, your car may not be worth your life, but your dignity is; and if it is not worth fight-ing for, it can hardly be said to exist.

The gift of life

Although difficult for modern man to fathom, it was once widely believed that life was a gift from God, that to not defend that life when offered violence was to hold God's gift in contempt, to be a coward and to breach one's duty to one's community. A sermon given in Philadelphia in 1747 unequivocally equated the failure to defend oneself with suicide:

"He that suffers his life to be taken from him by one that hath no authority for that purpose, when he might pre-

16

serve it by defense, incurs the Guilt of self murder since God hath enjoined him to seek the continuance of his life, and Nature itself teaches every creature to defend itself."

"Cowardice" and "self-respect" have largely disappeared from public discourse. In their place we are offered "self-esteem" as the bellwether of success and a proxy for dignity. "Self-respect" implies that one recognizes standards, and judges oneself worthy by the degree to which one lives up to them. "Self-esteem" simply means that one feels good about oneself. "Dignity" used to refer to the self-mastery and fortitude with which a person conducted himself in the face of life's vicissitudes and the boorish behavior of others. Now, judging by campus speech codes, it requires that we never encounter a discouraging word, and that others be coerced into acting respectfully, evidently on the assumption that we are powerless to prevent our degradation if exposed to the demeaning behavior of others. These are signposts proclaiming the insubstantiality of our character, the hollowness of our souls.

It is impossible to address the problem of rampant crime without talking about the moral responsibility of the intended victim. Crime is rampant because the law-abiding, each of us, condone it, excuse it, permit it, submit to it. We permit and encourage it because we do not fight back, immediately, then and there, where it happens. Crime is not rampant because we do not have enough prisons, because judges and prosecutors are too soft, because the police are hamstrung with absurd technicalities. The defect is there, in our character. We are a nation of cowards and shirkers.

Do you feel lucky?

In 1991 when then-Attorney General Richard Thornburgh released the FBI's crime statistics, he noted that it is now more likely that a person will be the victim of a violent crime in his lifetime than that he will be in an auto accident. Despite this, most people readily believe that the existence of the police relieves them of the responsibility to take full measures to protect themselves. The police, however, are not personal bodyguards. Rather, they act as a general deterrent to crime, both by their presence and by apprehending criminals after the fact. As numerous courts have held, they have no legal obligation to protect anyone in particular. You cannot sue them for failing to have prevented you from being the victim of a crime.

Insofar as the police deter by their presence, they are very, very good. Criminals take great pains to not commit a crime in front of them. Unfortunately, the corollary is that you can pretty much bet your life (and you are) that they won't be there at the moment you actually need them.

Should you ever be the victim of an assault, a robbery or a rape, you will find it very difficult to call the police while the act is in progress, even if you are carrying a portable cellular phone. Nevertheless, you might be interested to know how long it takes them to show up. Bureau of Justice Statistics for 1991 show that, for all crimes of violence, only 28% of the calls are responded to within five minutes. The idea that protection is a service that people can call to have delivered and expect to receive in a timely fashion is often mocked by gun owners, who love to recite the challenge, "Call for a cop, call for an ambulance, and call for a pizza. See who shows up first."

Many people deal with the problem of crime by convincing themselves that they live, work and travel only in special "crime-free" zones. Invariably, they react with shock and hurt surprise when they discover that criminals do not play by the rules and do not respect these imaginary boundaries. If, however, you understand that crime can occur anywhere at anytime, and if you understand that you can be maimed or mortally wounded in mere seconds, you may wish to consider whether you are willing to place the responsibility for safeguarding your life in the hands of others.

Power and responsibility

Is your life worth protecting? If so, whose responsibility is it to protect it? If you believe that it is the police's, not only are you wrong — since the courts universally rule that they have no legal obligation to do so — but you face some difficult moral quandaries. How can you rightfully ask another human being to risk his life to protect yours when you will assume no responsibility yourself? Because that is his job and we pay him to do it? Because your life is of incalculable value, but his is only worth the $30,000 yearly salary we pay him? If you believe it reprehensible to possess the means and will to use lethal force to repel a criminal assault, how can you call upon another to do so for you?

Do you believe that you are forbidden to protect yourself because the police are better qualified to protect you, because they know what they are doing but you're a rank amateur? Put aside that this is equivalent to believing that only concert pianists may play the piano and only professional athletes may play sports. What exactly are these special qualities possessed only by the police and other agents of the state and beyond the rest of us mere mortals?

One who values his life and takes seriously his responsibilities to his family and community will possess and cultivate the means of fighting back, and will retaliate when threatened with death or grievous bodily injury to himself or a loved one. He will never be content to rely solely on others for his safety, or to think he has done all that is possible by being aware of his surroundings and taking measures of avoidance. Let's not mince words. He will be armed, will be trained in the use of his weapon, and will defend himself when faced with lethal violence.

Fortunately, there is a weapon for preserving life and liberty that can be wielded effectively by almost anyone — the handgun. Small and light enough to be carried habitually, lethal, but unlike the knife or sword, not demanding great skill or strength to wield effectively, it truly is the "great equalizer." Requiring only hand-eye coordination and a modicum of ability to remain cool under pressure, it can be used effectively by the old and the weak against the young and the strong, by the one against the many.

The handgun is the only weapon that would give a lone female jogger a chance of prevailing against a gang of thugs intent on rape, a teacher a chance of protecting children at recess from a madman intent on massacring them, a family of tourists waiting at a mid-town subway station the means to protect themselves from a gang of teens armed with razors and knives.

But since we live in a society that by and large outlaws the carrying of arms, we are brought into the fray of the Great American Gun War. Gun control is one of the most prominent battlegrounds in our current culture wars. Yet it is unique in the half-heartedness with which our conservative leaders and pundits — our "conservative elite" — do battle, and have conceded the moral high ground to liberal gun control proponents. It is not a topic often written about, or written about with any great fervor, by William F. Buckley or Patrick Buchanan. As drug czar, William Bennett advised George Bush to ban "assault weapons". George Will is on record as recommending the repeal of the Second Amendment, and Jack Kemp is on record as favoring a ban on the possession of semi-automatic "assault weapons". The battle for gun rights is fought predominantly by the common man. The beliefs of both our liberal and conservative elites are in fact abetting the criminal rampage through our society.

Selling crime prevention

By any rational measure, nearly all gun control proposals are hokum. The Brady Bill, for example, would not have prevented John Hinckley from obtaining a gun to shoot President Reagan; he purchased his weapon five months before the attack and his medical records could not have served as a basis to deny his purchase of a gun since medical records are not public documents filed with the police. Similarly, California's waiting period and background check did not stop Patrick Purdy from purchasing the "assault rifle" and handguns he used to massacre children during recess in a Stockton schoolyard; the felony conviction that would have provided the basis for stopping the sales did not exist because Mr. Purdy's previous weapons violations were plea bargained down from felonies to misdemeanors.

In the mid-sixties there was a public service advertising campaign targeted at car owners about the prevention of car theft. The purpose of the ad was to urge car owners not to leave their keys in their car. The message was, "Don't help a good boy go bad." The implication was that, by leaving his car keys in his car, the normal, law-abiding car owner was contributing to the delinquency of minors who, if they just weren't tempted beyond their limits, would otherwise be "good". Now, in those days people still had a fair sense of just who was responsible for whose behavior. The ad succeeded in enraging a goodly portion of the populace, and was soon dropped.

Nearly all of the gun control measures offered by Handgun Control, Inc. (HCI) and its ilk embody the same bankrupt philosophy. They are founded on the belief that America's law-abiding gun-owners are the source of the problem. With their unholy desire for firearms, they are creating a society awash in a sea of guns, thereby helping good boys go bad, and helping bad boys be badder. This laying of moral blame for violent crime at the feet of the law-abiding, and the implicit absolution of the violent criminal for his misdeeds, naturally infuriates honest gun-owners.

The files of HCI and other gun-control organizations are filled with proposals to limit the availability of semiautomatic and other firearms to law-abiding citizens and barren of proposals for apprehending and punishing violent criminals. It is ludicrous to expect that the proposals of HCI, or any gun control laws, will significantly curb crime. According to Department of Justice and Bureau of Alcohol, Tobacco and Firearms (ATF) statistics, fully 90% of violent crimes are not committed with a handgun, and about 93% percent of guns obtained by violent criminals are not obtained through the lawful purchase and sale transactions that are the object of most gun-control legislation. Furthermore, the number of violent criminals is minute in comparison to the number of firearms owned by Americans — estimated by the ATF at about 200 million, approximately one-third of which are handguns. With so abundant a supply, there will always be enough guns available for those who wish to use them for nefarious ends, no matter how complete the legal prohibitions against them, or how draconian the punishment for their acquisition or use. No, the gun-control proposals of HCI and other gun-control organizations are not seriously intended as crime control. Something else is at work here.

The tyranny of the elite

Gun control is a moral crusade against a benighted, barbaric citizenry. This is demonstrated not only by the ineffectualness of gun control in preventing crime, and by the fact that it focuses on restricting the behavior of the law-abiding rather than apprehending and punishing the guilty, but also by the execration that gun-control proponents heap on gun-owners and their evil instrumentality, the NRA. Gun-owners are routinely portrayed as uneducated, paranoid rednecks fascinated by and prone to violence, i.e., exactly the type of person who opposes the liberal agenda and whose moral and social "re-education" is the object of liberal social policies. Typical of such bigotry is New York Gov. Mario Cuomo's famous characterization of gun-owners as "hunters who drink beer, don't vote and lie to their wives about where they were all weekend." Similar vituperation is rained upon the NRA, characterized by Sen. Edward Kennedy as the "pusher's best friend", lampooned in political cartoons as standing for the right of children to carry firearms to school and, in general, portrayed as standing for an individual's God-given right to blow people away at will.

The stereotype is, of course, false. As criminologist and constitutional lawyer Don B. Kates and former HCI contributor Dr. Patricia Harris have pointed out, "[s]tudies consistently show that, on the average, gun owners are better educated and have more prestigious jobs than non-owners . . . . Later studies show that gun owners are *less* likely than non-owners to approve of police brutality, violence against dissenters, etc."

Conservatives must understand that the antipathy many liberals have for gun owners arises in good measure from their statist utopianism. This habit of mind has nowhere been better explored than in *The Republic*. There, Plato demonstrates that the perfectly just society is one in which an unarmed people exhibit virtue by minding their own business in the performance of their assigned functions, while the government of philosopher-kings, above the law and protected by armed guardians unquestioning in their loyalty to the state, engineers, implements and fine tunes the creation

22

of that society, aided and abetted by myths that both hide and justify their totalitarian manipulation.

The unarmed life

When columnist Carl Rowan preaches gun control and uses a gun to defend his home, when Maryland Gov. William Donald Schaefer seeks legislation year after year to ban semiautomatic "assault weapons" whose only purpose, we are told, is to kill people, while he is at the same time escorted by state police armed with large-capacity 9mm semiautomatic pistols, it is not simple hypocrisy. It is the workings of that habit of mind possessed by all superior beings who have taken upon themselves the terrible burden of civilizing the masses and who understand, like our Congress, that laws are for other people.

The liberal elite know that they are philosopher-kings. They know that the people simply cannot be trusted; that they are incapable of just and fair self-government; that left to their own devices, their society will be racist, sexist, homophobic and inequitable; and the liberal elite know how to fix things. They are going to help us live the good and just life, even if they have to lie to us and force us to do it. And they detest those who stand in their way.

The private ownership of firearms is a rebuke to this utopian zeal. To own firearms is to affirm that freedom and liberty are not gifts from the state. It is to reserve final judgment about whether the state is encroaching on freedom and liberty, to stand ready to defend that freedom with more than mere words, and stand outside the state's totalitarian reach.

The Florida experience

The elitist distrust of the people underlying the gun control movement is illustrated beautifully in HCI's campaign against a new concealed-carry law in Florida. Prior to 1987, the Florida law permitting the issuance of concealed carry permits was administered at the county level. The law was vague and, as a result, was subject to conflicting interpretation and political manipulation. Permits were valid only within the county of issuance.

23

In 1987, Florida enacted a uniform concealed carry permit law which mandates that county authorities issue a permit to anyone who satisfies certain objective criteria. The law requires that a permit be issued to any applicant who is a resident, at least 21 years of age, has no criminal record, no record of alcohol or drug abuse, no history of mental illness, and provides evidence of having satisfactorily completed a firearms safety course offered by the NRA or other competent instructor. The applicant must provide a set of fingerprints, after which the authorities make a background check. The permit must be issued or denied within ninety days, is valid throughout the state, and must be renewed every three years, which provides authorities a regular means of reevaluating whether the permit holder still qualifies.

Passage of this legislation was vehemently opposed by HCI and the media. The law, they said, would lead to citizens shooting each other over everyday disputes involving fender benders, impolite behavior and other slights to their dignity. Terms like "Florida, the Gunshine State", and "Dodge City East" were coined to suggest that the state, and those seeking passage of the law, were encouraging individuals to act as judge, jury and executioner in a "Death Wish" society.

No HCI campaign more clearly demonstrates the elitist beliefs underlying the campaign to eradicate gun-ownership. Given the qualifications required of permit holders, HCI and the media can only believe that common, law-abiding citizens are seething cauldrons of homicidal rage, ready to kill to avenge any slight to their dignity, eager to seek out and summarily execute the lawless. Only lack of immediate access to a gun restrains them and prevents the blood from flowing in the streets. They are so mentally and morally deficient that they would mistake a permit to carry a weapon in self-defense as a state-sanctioned license to kill at will.

Did the dire predictions come true? Despite the fact that Miami and Dade County have severe problems with the drug trade, the homicide rate fell in Florida following enactment of this law, as it also did in Oregon following enactment of similar legislation there.

There are, in addition, several documented cases of new permit holders successfully using their weapons to defend themselves. Information from the Florida Department of State shows that, from the beginning of the program in 1987 through June, 1993, 160,823 permits have been issued, and only 530, or about 0.33% of the applicants, have been denied a permit for failure to satisfy the criteria, indicating that the law is benefiting those whom it was intended to benefit — the law-abiding. Only 16 permits, less than 1/100th of 1%, have been revoked due to the post-issuance commission of a crime involving a firearm.

The Florida legislation has been used as a model for legislation adopted by Oregon, Idaho, Montana and Mississippi. In addition, there are seven other states (Maine, North and South Dakota, Utah, Washington, West Virginia and, with the exception of cities with a population in excess of 1 million, Pennsylvania) which provide that concealed carry permits must be issued to law-abiding citizens who satisfy various objective criteria. Finally, no permit is required at all in Vermont. Altogether, then, there are thirteen states in which law-abiding citizens who wish to carry arms to defend themselves may do so. While no one appears to have compiled the statistics from all of these jurisdictions, there is certainly an ample data base for those seeking the truth about the trustworthiness of law-abiding citizens who carry firearms.

Other evidence also suggests that armed citizens are very responsible in using guns to defend themselves. Florida State University criminologist Gary Kleck, using surveys and other data, has determined that armed citizens defend their lives or property with firearms against criminals approximately 1 million times a year. In ninety-eight percent of these instances, the citizen merely brandishes the weapon or fires a warning shot. Only in 2 percent of the cases do citizens actually shoot their assailants. In defending themselves with their firearms, armed citizens kill 2,000 to 3,000 criminals each year, three times the number killed by police. A nationwide comparative study by Kates, the constitutional lawyer and criminologist, found that only about 2 percent of civilian shootings involved an innocent person mistakenly identified as a criminal. The "error rate" for the police, however was 11%, over five times as high.

It is simply not possible to square the above numbers and the experience of Florida with the notions that honest, law-abiding gun-owners are borderline psychopaths itching for an excuse to shoot someone, vigilantes eager to seek out and summarily execute the lawless, or incompetent fools incapable of determining when it is proper to use lethal force in defense of their lives. Nor upon reflection should these results seem surprising. Rape, robbery and attempted murder are typically not actions rife with ambiguity or subtlety, requiring educated powers of observation and great book learning to discern. When a man pulls a knife on a woman and says, "You're coming with me", her judgment that a crime is being committed is not likely to be in error. There is little chance that she is going to shoot the wrong person. It is the police, because they are rarely if ever at the scene of the crime when it occurs, who are more likely to find themselves in circumstances where guilt and innocence are not so clear-cut, and in which the probability for mistakes is higher.

Arms and liberty

Classical republican philosophy has long recognized the critical relationship between personal liberty and the possession of arms by a people ready and willing to use them. Political theorists as dissimilar as Niccolo Machiavelli, Sir Thomas More, James Harrington, Algernon Sidney, John Locke, and Jean-Jacques Rousseau all shared the view that possession of arms is vital for resisting tyranny, and that to be disarmed by one's government is tantamount to being enslaved by it. The possession of arms by the people is the ultimate warrant that government governs only with the consent of the governed. As Kates has shown, the Second Amendment is as much a product of this political philosophy as it is of the American experience in the Revolutionary War. Yet our conservative elite has abandoned this aspect of republican political theory. Although our conservative pundits recognize and embrace gun-owners as allies in other arenas, their battle for gun rights is desultory. The problem here is not a statist utopianism, although goodness knows that liberals are not alone in the confidence they have in the state's ability to solve society's problems. Rather, the problem seems to lie in certain cultural traits shared by our conservative and liberal elites.

One such trait is an abounding faith in the power of the word. The failure of our conservative elite to defend the Second Amendment stems in great measure from an overestimation of the power of the rights set forth in the First Amendment, and a general undervaluation of action. Implicit in calls for the repeal of the Second Amendment is the assumption that our First Amendment rights are sufficient to preserve our liberty. The belief is that liberty can be preserved as long as men freely speak their minds; that there is no tyranny or abuse that can survive being exposed in the press; and that the truth need only be disclosed for the culprits to be shamed. The people will act, and the truth shall set us, and keep us, free.

History is not kind to this belief, tending rather to support the views of Hobbes, Machiavelli and other republican theorists that only people willing and able to defend themselves can preserve their liberties. While it may be tempting and comforting to believe that the existence of mass electronic communication has forever altered the balance of power between the state and its subjects, the belief has certainly not been tested by time, and what little history there is in the age of mass communication is not especially encouraging. The camera, radio and press are mere tools and, like guns, can be used for good or ill. Hitler, after all, was a masterful orator, used radio to very good effect, and is well known to have pioneered and exploited the propaganda opportunities afforded by film. And then, of course, there were the Brownshirts, who knew very well how to quell dissent among intellectuals.

Polite society

In addition to being enamored of the power of words, our conservative elite shares with liberals the notion that an armed society is just not civilized or progressive, that massive gun ownership

27

is a blot on our civilization. This association of personal disarmament with civilized or polite behavior is one of the great unexamined beliefs of our times.

Should you read English literature from the sixteenth through nineteenth centuries, you will discover numerous references to the fact that a gentleman, especially when out at night or traveling, armed himself with a sword or a pistol against the chance of encountering a highwayman or other such predator. This does not appear to have shocked the ladies accompanying him. True, for the most part there were no police in those days, but we have already addressed the notion that the presence of the police absolves people of the responsibility to look after their safety, and in any event the existence of the police cannot be said to have reduced crime to negligible levels.

It is by no means obvious why it is "civilized" to permit oneself to fall easy prey to criminal violence, and to permit criminals to continue unobstructed in their evil ways. While it may be that a society in which crime is so rare that no one ever needs to carry a weapon is "civilized", a society which stigmatizes the carry of weapons by the law-abiding — because it distrusts its citizens more than it fears rapists, robbers and murderers — certainly cannot claim this distinction. Perhaps the notion that defending oneself with lethal force is not "civilized" arises from the view that violence is always wrong, or that each human being is of such intrinsic worth that it is wrong to kill anyone under any circumstances. The necessary implication of these propositions, however, is that life is not worth defending. Far from being "civilized", the beliefs that counterviolence and killing are always wrong are an invitation to the spread of barbarism. Such beliefs announce loudly and clearly that those who do not respect the lives and property of others will rule over those who do.

In truth, one who believes it wrong to arm himself against criminal violence shows contempt of God's gift of life (or in modern parlance, does not properly value himself), does not live up to his responsibilities to his family or community, and proclaims himself mentally and morally deficient, believing that he cannot trust himself to behave responsibly. In truth, a state that deprives its law-abiding citizens of the means to effectively defend themselves is not civilized but barbarous, becoming an accomplice of murderers, rapists and thugs and revealing its totalitarian nature by its tacit admission that the disorganized, random havoc created by criminals is far less a threat than are men and women who believe themselves free and independent, and act accordingly.

While gun-control proponents and other advocates of a kinder, gentler society incessantly decry our "armed society," in truth we do not live in an armed society. We live in a society in which violent criminals and agents of the state habitually carry weapons, and in which many of our law-abiding citizens own firearms but do not go about armed. Department of Justice Statistics indicate that nearly 87 percent of all violent crime occurs *outside* the home. Essentially, although tens of millions own firearms, we are an unarmed society.

Take back the night

Clearly the police and the courts are not providing a significant brake on criminal activity. While liberals call for more poverty, education, and drug treatment programs, conservatives take a more direct tack. George Will advocates a massive increase in the number of police and a shift towards "community based policing." The NRA and many conservative leaders call for laws that would require violent criminals serve at least 85 percent of their sentences and place repeat offenders permanently behind bars.

Our society suffers greatly from the beliefs that only official action is legitimate and that the state is the source of our earthly salvation. Both liberal and conservative prescriptions for curbing violent crime suffer from the "not in my job description" school of thought regarding the responsibilities of the law-abiding citizen, and from an overestimation of the ability of the state to provide society's moral moorings. As long as law-abiding citizens assume no personal responsibility for combating crime, liberal and conservative programs will fail to contain it.

Judging from the numerous articles about concealed-carry in gun magazines, the growing number of products advertised for such purpose, and the increase in the number of concealed-carry permit applications in states with mandatory issuance laws, more and more people, including growing numbers of women, are carrying firearms for self-defense. Since many live in states where the issuance of permits is discretionary, and in which law enforcement officials routinely deny applications, many people have been put to the hard choice between protecting their lives or respecting the law. Some of these people have learned the hard way, by being a victim of a crime, or by seeing a friend or loved one raped, robbed or murdered, that violent crime can happen to anyone, anywhere at anytime, and that crime is not about sex or property, but life, liberty and dignity.

The laws proscribing the concealed carry of firearms by honest, law-abiding citizens breed nothing but disrespect for the law. As the Founding Fathers knew well, a government that does not trust its honest, law-abiding, taxpaying citizens with the means of self-defense, is not itself worthy of trust. Laws disarming honest citizens proclaim that the government is the master, not the servant, of the people. A federal law along the lines of the Florida statute — overriding all contradictory state and local laws and acknowledging that the carry of firearms by law-abiding citizens is a privilege and immunity of citizenship — is needed to correct the outrageous conduct of state and local officials o₁ ·rating under discretionary licensing systems.

What we certainly do not need is more gun control. Those who call for the repeal of the Second Amendment so that we can really begin controlling firearms betray a serious misunderstanding of the Bill of Rights. The Bill of Rights does not *grant* rights to the people, such that its repeal would legitimately confer upon government the powers otherwise proscribed. The Bill of Rights is the list of the fundamental, inalienable rights, endowed in man by his Creator, that define what it means to be a free and independent people, the rights which must exist to insure that government governs only with the consent of the people.

At one time this was understood even by the Supreme Court. In *United States v. Cruikshank* (1876), the first case in which the Supreme Court had the opportunity to interpret the Second Amendment, the Court stated that the right confirmed by the Second Amendment "is not a right granted by the constitution. Neither is it in any manner dependent upon that instrument for its existence." The repeal of the Second Amendment would no more render the outlawing of firearms legitimate than the repeal of the due process clause of the Fifth Amendment would authorize the government to imprison and kill people at will. A government that abrogates any of the Bill of Rights, with or without majoritarian approval, forever acts illegitimately, becomes tyrannical, and loses the moral right to govern.

This is the uncompromising understanding reflected in the warning that America's gun owners will not go gently into that good, utopian night: "You can have my gun when you pry it from my cold, dead hands." While liberals take this statement as evidence of the retrograde, violent nature of gun owners, we gun owners hope that liberals hold equally strong sentiments about their printing presses, word processors and television cameras. The republic depends upon fervent devotion to all our fundamental rights.

A License To Save Your Life?

The day after Colin Ferguson opened fire with a 9mm handgun on the Long Island Railroad, leaving six dead and 17 wounded, Handgun Control, Inc. issued its new, proposed legislation calling for nationwide licensing of gun owners, stating that it "will help provide a solution to America's epidemic of gun violence." President Clinton has echoed the need for this law, and has directed the Justice Department to begin studying the licensing proposal.

According to HCI, we should implement a licensing and registration system for handguns similar to the automobile licensing system "because handguns are more dangerous than automobiles. While cars kill by accident, handguns kill because they are designed and intended to do so." HCI thus proposes that a license be required to purchase or transfer a handgun and to purchase handgun ammunition. To obtain the license, the individual would have to:

- be at least 21 years old,
- present proof of residency,
- go through fingerprint and name-based background checks,

- complete a safety training course,
- present proof of liability insurance coverage to ensure compensation of victims of negligent handgun misuse, and
- pay a fee to cover the cost of the license.

Do President Clinton and HCI truly believe that violent crime runs rampant in this country because criminals do not know the rules of safe gun handling, lack technical proficiency with their firearms, do not carry insurance to compensate the innocent, unintended victims of their drive-by shootings, or simply do not know that murdering someone is against the law?

Are we actually to believe that a licensing system that insures that gunmen know how to avoid accidents, are marksmen who will hit only what they intend to hit, and pass a written exam where they correctly answer that using a gun to rape, rob or murder is against the law will reduce violent crime? Are we actually to believe that rampant violent crime can be curbed by a requirement that handgun owners be subject to an *administrative procedure*?

Obviously, criminals will no more obey licensing laws than they obey the far more fundamental laws against rape, robbery and murder. But even ignoring this fact, the HCI licensing system cannot possibly reduce violent crime. The responsible use of a firearm depends on the moral character of the individual who wields the weapon, and not on his technical proficiency. If a person is not restrained by an absolute sense of right and wrong, no amount of technical training in the use of firearms, or memorization and recitation of the criminal laws, will provide the moral sense he lacks.

The Clinton administration and HCI know this, and their proposal that an automobile-style licensing system for gun owners will reduce crime is, at best, disingenuous. When President Clinton talks of setting standards that individuals would have to meet to be eligible to own a gun, he means not only to erect significant administrative and cost barriers to the acquisition of firearms by law-abiding citizens, but, more fundamentally, to set up the government as the judge of an individual's "need" to own a gun.

This, of course, converts the constitutional right to own firearms in to a privilege granted and administered by the government. Crime can happen to anyone, anywhere, at any time. Thus, a government that arrogates to itself the power to judge, in the first instance, your "need" or "eligibility" to own a gun can only believe that your life is not really worth protecting, at least until such time as you present strong proof to the contrary; or the government is planning on basing that determination on something other than the value of your life to you or your loved ones. It is certainly not a government that believes that you have an inalienable right to life.

Like the Brady Bill before it, the HCI licensing proposal is principally an exercise in social piety. The licensing system will apply only to the law-abiding who believe it their duty to comply with the laws. To the extent it is successful, it prevents the lawless from acquiring their arms through lawful channels. Its proponents may, therefore, sleep better at night knowing that society is not morally tainted by unwittingly assisting the lawless, and that criminals can obtain their weapons only through the black market. While this may be a great source of comfort to them, it will no more curb violent crime than the system for obtaining prescription drugs curbs the market for, and use of, illegal drugs.

Whether it be licensing or banning guns, creating poverty and drug treatment programs, building more prisons or abolishing parole, our fearless leaders view crime from a relentlessly utilitarian perspective, as a question solely of arranging matters to secure the greatest safety for the greatest number. There is only one approach to the problem of crime, however, that respects the fact that *each* individual has an inalienable right to life and liberty and a moral right and obligation to defend himself: legalizing the carrying of arms.

Without that, every other "solution" asks that we abide our helplessness and tolerate the sacrificial status of our lives and liberty, until our government, like an alchemist seeking the incantations and procedures that transmute lead into gold, succeeds in enacting the laws that transform our society into that bright and shining city on the hill.

Despite all the New Age psychobabble about government programs to "empower" the people, decriminalizing the carrying of arms by law-abiding citizens is on no one's agenda, and remains unthinkable. Following the LIRR shooting, Mr. Clinton told a group of mayors and police chiefs that he believes that the country "is really prepared in a way that it has not been before . . . to do something about violent crime."

He means, however, that the people are prepared to let the government enact more sweeping restraints on otherwise lawful behavior in the hope of preventing crime, so that they themselves will not have to do anything about crime.

He means that enough people now believe that if they turn enough of their rights into privileges granted and administered by the government, subject to the approval and supervision of bureaucrats who know more and care more than they themselves about their lives, their families and their communities, they will live happier, safer, more productive lives.

Sadly, judging by opinion polls favoring licensing and other restrictions on firearms and by the eagerness of our legislators to "do something" about crime, the President may be right. But those of us who do not believe that our society suffers from rampant crime and other ills because we have not yet given government enough power over our lives, those of us who are not waiting for the police or laws and government programs to save us, we must carry arms. Everywhere and at all times.

It little matters whether the risk of criminal victimization is one in a hundred or one in million, for the statistical risk of victimization provides neither the necessity nor the moral or legal justification for carrying arms. Your life is worth protecting at all times and places, not just occasionally or in the home. Besides, as Jeff Cooper, the nation's leading firearms instructor, has noted, "statistics are cold comfort when you discover that your case is the rare exception."

We must carry arms. Not because we are frightened of crime. Not because it is an unfortunate necessity of modern life. We must carry arms because we value our lives and those of our loved ones, because we will not be dealt with by force or threat of force, and do not live at the pleasure and discretion of the lawless.

Failing that, and while we wait for laws to restrain men, we will be condemned to wonder why criminals have no respect for our lives, when we ourselves do not value our lives enough to assume the responsibility to defend them. For surely as long as we do not hold our lives worth fighting for, we hold God's great gift — life — in contempt, and God Himself will not save us.

GUNS AND FEMINISM

The May 1994 Ms. magazine bears on its cover a 9mm Smith & Wesson and asks, "Is This Power Feminism?" Inside, an article, "Living With Guns, Playing With Fire," by Ann Jones, author of *Women Who Kill* and *Next Time She'll Be Dead: Battering and How to Stop It*, provides feminist commentary on the fact that increasing numbers of women are buying guns and the view, expressed by feminist author Naomi Wolfe, that these women represent a new form of "power feminism." In criticizing these developments, Ms. Jones provides the feminist orthodoxy's latest installment in its ongoing series, Why Guns Are Not The Answer.

Ms. Jones begins by noting that, while the fear inspired by random violence is spurring a national debate about, and crackdown on, crime, the greatest threat to women's safety is not random violence by strangers, but murder, rape and assaults by current or former husbands or boyfriends. "Battering is now the single leading cause of injury to U.S. women between the ages of 15 and 44," writes Ms. Jones, "sending more than a million women every year to doctors' offices or emergency rooms for treatment."

Enter, says Ms. Jones, the NRA, with its new campaign, "Refuse to be a Victim," an adept marketing ploy designed to tap into women's fears of random violence and play to ". . . the real terror of millions of U.S. women who are still victimized by men who are their partners or lovers."

By couching its campaign in "the feminist language of choice," the NRA seeks to exploit ". . . the sentiments of those women who extol women's power and reject what they call `victim feminism.'" Don't think, warns Ms. Jones, that the NRA has women's best interests at heart. The proof? "During recent campaigns in several states for legislation authorizing police to confiscate guns from men who assault women or violate restraining orders, the NRA said *nothing*."

No, the NRA's campaign is designed solely to garner new funds and to raise membership rolls by manipulating women with false promises of empowerment.

Real empowerment, evidently, would be passing laws to insure that, when that abusive husband or boyfriend wanted to murder you, he would have to use a baseball bat or a knife, run you down with his car, or strangle you, so that you would not have to suffer the special indignity of being murdered with a gun.

Ms. Jones warns us that women's interest in guns may not be just about fear, but also about getting even. Lorena Bobbit, she notes, certainly "refused to be a victim." The widespread cheering and laughter by women at her act (cutting off her husband's penis while he slept) revealed "a vein of vengefulness, a mother lode of anger, a vast buildup of unrequited insults and injuries." As further evidence, she cites the fact that women watching *Thelma and Louise* cheer when Louise shoots the would-be rapist after preventing him from raping Thelma, but when he persists in taunting Louise.

It is not clear where Ms. Jones is going with this. Perhaps she means to frighten both men and women with the notion that women may use guns to get even. As Lorena Bobbit showed, however, you don't need a gun if revenge is what you're after. Vengeance can bide its time.

Perhaps, though, she means to suggest that women, having been oppressed too long and endured too many indignities, cannot be trusted with guns, and should not trust themselves with guns, because they will hysterically or gleefully "overreact" when their safety is threatened.

As an illustration of the shortcomings of the criminal justice system and the potential uselessness of guns, Ms. Jones relates the story of April LaSalata, whose ex-husband broke into her Long Island home and stabbed her several times in the chest. She survived and her ex-husband was charged with attempted murder, but released on $25,000 bail.

Ms. LaSalata applied for a permit to carry a firearm, but was denied. Shortly thereafter, the ex, lying in wait outside her home, shot Ms. LaSalata twice in the head. Had Ms. LaSalata been granted the permit, could she have saved herself? Maybe so, Ms. Jones answers, but also maybe not.

Then follows the litany of why gun ownership may not be an unadulterated good. If you have a gun, it may be fatal for you if you're on the losing end of a struggle with an intruder. By having a gun in the house, an abusive husband or boyfriend may use it on you. A child may accidentally kill himself or another. Any family member may use it to commit suicide.

Arguments such as these are commonly made by gun-control proponents as reasons not to own a gun. At bottom, such arguments rest on the craven suggestion that you ought not to fight back unless you are first guaranteed perfect, risk-free protection.

Guns are mere tools, however, and no tool can be operated free of the possibility of human error or misuse, and all tools have limitations. These facts, however, do not render them any less useful or suitable for their intended purposes in the proper circumstances.

The argument that a gun is useless because in a particular circumstance you might not be able to use it in time, or it might not save you, is no less nonsensical than the argument that there is no point owning or using a seat belt, since if you collide head on with a tractor trailer, it will not save you, and in some cases it might be better if you were thrown clear.

Similarly, the fact that "it might be used against you" is true of any tool, since the use of a tool depends on the purpose of the person wielding it. A recent syndicated column by Mike Royko pointed out, for example, that a number of murders in Chicago had been committed by drowning the victims in toilets. Ms. Jones could with equal force assert, "Bring a toilet into the home, and he might use it against you."

Or a pen, a scissors, a lamp, a pillow, a chair, a bat.

Short of re-bioengineering the human race, men, who are on average bigger and stronger than women, will never lack for a means of killing, maiming or beating women. Women will, however, lack the most effective means to deprive men of these advantages if they cannot and do not own firearms.

Ms. Jones does not rest her argument, however, solely on the fact that guns cannot provide perfect, risk-free protection. At bottom, real power feminism is, in her view, to bring about and rely on a just and powerful government that cares enough about women to prevent violence from befalling them:

> "[H]ow do we stop violent men? That's not a job to be done piecemeal by lone women, armed with pearl-handled pistols, picking off batterers and rapists one by one. It's a job for the collective power of women and men. It should never be up to the April LaSalatas of the world to arm themselves and shoot it out with men who are trying to kill them. The law could have saved April, and should have, and would have, if women mattered . . . I'm all for empowering victims . . . [but] when we took up the fight for women's rights, the right to bear arms was not what we had in mind. We imagined a just country in which

cops and courts would defend, if need be, a woman's constitutional right to be free from bodily harm."

Thus, real "power feminism" turns out to be collective action to bring about a society in which women do not have to assume the responsibility to defend themselves because they can rely on others who really care about women, i.e., cops, to risk their own lives to protect them from violence, and the courts to restrain and put away violent men.

Evidently feminine helplessness is acceptable as part of feminist dogma if women rely on a just, egalitarian and caring state as their protector rather than on an individual, unreliable and sexist man. Evidently feminist dogma requires some people, such as cops, to stand ready to dispense lethal violence to protect women, so that women need not sully their own moral purity by taking up arms, or face or bear the logical consequences of their pacifism.

In Ms. Jones' view, individuals are not independent forces of law and order in society. She cannot conceive, as acceptable, any response to male violence against women that relies on "lone women . . . picking off batters and rapists one by one." In her view, women who defend themselves act only for themselves, and cannot alter the nature of the society they live in. It is the state which is the ultimate repository for, and has the sole capability to implement and change, society's values. Progress is made by convincing cops, courts and the government that women "matter."

By focusing on guns, she has, however, missed the point of women taking up arms. Ms. Jones is quite right in her basic argument that guns are not the "solution" to male violence against women. but for quite the wrong reasons. Guns are mere tools which may be used for good or ill, their mere existence signifying, and capable of accomplishing, nothing. It is the resolve to not tolerate criminal victimization, coupled with the will to defend oneself by any and all necessary means that will prove far more daunting to criminals than efforts to convince the government that women "matter."

And while feminist leaders are busy petitioning government to change a sexist society and deal decisively with violent men, women may wish to question the peculiar nature of an equality, independence and freedom that depend, for their very existence, on reliance on state action rather than their own resources and capabilities. What the government gives, the government can take away.

THE ETHICS OF THE RIGHT TO KEEP AND BEAR ARM

Speech presented to
Les Amis de la Liberté
Montreal, Canada
August 3, 1996

Introduction

I want to thank Pierre Lemieux, Marie Latourelle and Les Amis de la Liberté for inviting me to Montreal to address the ethics of the right to keep and bear arms. This kindness and generosity is all the more impressive because gun control is not generally regarded, so I hear, as a very interesting or important topic among Canadians. And, if I am to believe my Canadian friends, the American love-affair with guns is regarded here as fairly incomprehensible, and we Americans are viewed as wild-eyed cowboys, madmen or barbarians.

Perhaps, however, you have been watching too many American movies and television shows. Perhaps our two nations are not as far apart as you might think. If you look at the first page of the handout I have distributed to you, you will see an article from this week's New York Times reporting that it has just been made legal to purchase and carry chemical mace for self-defense in New York. It is an interesting article, and in it you will see that the various public officials involved anguished over making this decision.

Please note that we are talking about a product here that causes no permanent injury, has an effective range of about 10 feet, and is launched from an aerosol can, so that if the wind is blowing the wrong way when the defender is attacked, the spray will be blown back into his face. Some of the statements made in this article are quite revealing about American attitudes:

1. Governor Pataki, in signing the bill, said that "By legalizing self-defense sprays we are empowering the people of New York with this safe and legal means of self-protection." Thus, you see, we Americans understand that government is the source of our personal power, and that our right to self-protection is bestowed upon us by government.

2. The Mayor of New York City, who opposed the law, said that "One has only to contemplate the danger of an inappropriate discharge of a self-defense spray in a crowded rush-hour subway car in order to imagine the potential for disaster contained in this bill." Thus you see that we Americans have a very highly refined sense of what constitutes a "disaster," and a very high risk aversion to anything that has a potential for creating disasters of this magnitude.

3. Worries about the competence and trustworthiness of citizens abound. The Mayor worries about an "inappropriate discharge." Law-enforcement officials said they had concerns about placing such weapons in the hands of *ordinary* citizens." The Police Commissioner of New York City expressed concerns that the sprays might "be misused by citizens who lack proper training."

4. In contrast to the suspect competency and trustworthiness of "ordinary citizens," the competency and trustworthiness of the police, nominally our servants, and their privileged position as expert authorities on what should be permitted to "ordinary citizens," is assumed and unquestionable.

5. The article points out that the police did not object to the new law once the legislators agreed to make use of the sprays against a police officer a felony, thus recognizing the officers' special, protected and elevated status.

So you see, I hope, that many Americans have a correct understanding of the right of ordinary people to protect themselves, and are not, perhaps, the madmen or wild cowboys you may think us to be. And I hope that I have now done my small part to show you that our two great peoples are closer in our thoughts on personal liberty than you may have been led to believe.

The right to keep and bear arms

Before beginning a discussion of ethics, allow me to present a quick summary of the standard, libertarian derivation of the right to keep and bear arms. It is fairly simply stated:

1. Each individual owns his life, or has a right to his life.

2. The right to life of necessity implies that the individual has a right to protect, or defend that life.

3. The right to defend one's life is meaningless, or a hollow promise, unless that right also encompasses the right to the means necessary for the effective exercise of that right.

   Thus, for example, the fundamental right of free speech would be relatively meaningless if it only encompassed the right to speak one's mind wherever one happened to be or to stand in a public park and broadcast one's opinions to the people within listening distance. The right has been rendered meaningful, full-bodied and effective by protection of the *freedom of the press*, that is, by protection of the instrumentality by which one in fact exercises the individual right within society.

4. Since the right to life implies a right to the means to protect that life, the individual's right to his own life necessarily implies a right to keep and bear arms suitable for self-defense. In this place and time, that means the handgun, small enough to be habitually carried almost at all times.

5. A government of a free people is instituted, as it says in the American Declaration of Independence, only with the consent of the governed, in order to secure each person's right to life. Such a government must, of necessity, therefore, recognize the right of the people to keep and bear their private arms for

defense. The right of the people to keep and bear arms is the ultimate warrant that government governs only with the consent of the governed, for the people retain the means of revolt and resistance to brute, tyrannical force. The individual right to keep and bear arms is the ultimate recognition by the government that government is the servant of the people and not its master. To keep and bear arms is to affirm that rights and liberty are not gifts from the state.

This completes our overview of the libertarian derivation of the right to bear arms.

I would like to make one final point, however, about the paradoxical nature of the legal protection of fundamental rights — whether it be free speech or the right to life. Man is a synthesis of the finite and the infinite, spirit and matter. We cannot protect the right to freedom of thought *per se*; it is invisible and intangible. We can only protect the concrete means of its expression, the means and tools by which the word enters the world, becomes flesh and dwells among us. And so our First Amendment protects, not freedom of thought, but freedom of the press.

Similarly, laws cannot protect the spirit that loves liberty and resists tyranny, or the indomitable spirit that refuses to accede to enslavement or criminal victimization by another, summed up in the simple phrase, "right to life." That spirit is intangible and invisible; that spirit cannot be created by law, nor can it be protected by law per se. We can only lay hold of and protect the physical means by which that spirit expresses itself and becomes concrete, namely, the act of self-defense, and the tools of self-defense. And so our Second Amendment protects not "the right to life," or "self-determination," but the right to keep and bear arms.

Here is the paradox. The printing press, and firearms, are in fact only tools; their use depends on the purpose and character of the user. They contain within themselves nothing which vouchsafes their employment only in the service of the good, or to the greater good of mankind. That depends entirely on the character of the people, and their willingness to act upon their beliefs.

48

As tools, they can be, and are, used for both good and ill. This is obvious in the case of handguns, but it is equally true for the press, though less often taken note of. Hitler's advancement was due in notable part to the popular appeal of a book — *Mein Kampf*. The press, and here I include radio, television and the cinema, may be readily employed for propaganda purposes, to mislead rather than to inform, and, in its form as entertainment, to divert people's attention from their plight — part of the time-honored strategy of "bread and circuses".

This paradox, or tension, that we cannot protect what we value in man except through protection of the physical means of its expression, yet as tools their value is completely neutral or ambiguous, is the source of much of the debate over the value of so-called "individual rights," and the extent to which it is permissible to restrict those rights.

The ethics of bearing arms

A great deal of the debate over the right to keep and bear arms has to do with the propositions, and chain of reasoning and the problems associated with the paradoxical nature of affording legal protection to the physical means of exercising fundamental rights I just summarized. I wanted to give you a quick review of the derivation of the right to keep and bear arms, however, not to give you a course in individual rights theology, but because I want you to keenly appreciate the difference between that subject and the one I am now going to discuss now: ethics.

It may seem at first that ethics and rights are so closely related that they can only be discussed together. Perhaps that is so, as some people conceive ethics as the rules of right or wrong for interpersonal relations.

That is not, however, what I mean by ethics. Ethics, as I will speak about it, has to do with the resolve one makes to *act* based upon one's relation to God or, if that word conjures images in your mind of a large, stern, white-haired gentleman in the sky, then as one's relation to the *eternal*.

Whether we call them "individual rights," or "human rights," all rights in the political and legal sense of the word are social conventions or social sanctions. To have a right is to be recognized, certainly by law and hopefully by the better portion of one's fellow citizens, to be privileged to act within a certain domain without harassment by the laws and, hopefully, the adverse opinion of one's fellow citizens. To have a right is to have a privileged domain of action in which one need fear neither punishment, nor the loss of comity or good will of fellow citizens.

From the standpoint of an individual's relation to God, or the eternal, however, the fact that the law, or the opinion of our fellow citizens, does or does not permit us to act in certain way, does not let us off the hook — we remain responsible for our choices and our conduct. Fear of the consequences does not excuse shrinking away from doing what is right, that is, what in good conscience is absolutely required. Ethics, in other words, disdains this method of deciding one's course of action based on the probable consequences — the outcome.

Ethically speaking, then, the question is not what is or should be permitted, or to put it less charitably, what will my fellow citizens let me get away with, but what is right to do? How am I, in good conscience before eternity, required to act? What is *absolutely required* of me?

I choose for our consideration a sudden, violent assault that imminently threatens your life or great bodily harm. What is the right course of action? How should one act so that one may bear the judgment of one's conscience, God, and all eternity, and not merely be either praised or excused in the eyes of one's fellow man? I propose for consideration the following resolve: to resist with all your heart, body, mind, and very soul.

To evaluate this proposed answer, let us undertake a series of what in American high schools is called, "values clarification exercises." Please turn to the second page of the handout I have distributed. There you will see a graphic presentation of the U.S. homicide rate for 1900-1994. You will note that Americans began the century with a very low rate of around 1 per 100,000, which increased to a high point of 9.7 per 100,000 in 1933, when Prohibition was repealed. That year began a long period of decline that continued at low rates through the 1950s until the mid-1960s, when the rate began to sharply increase again, reaching a high point of 10.2 per 100,000 in 1980. The rate has been at or above 8/100,000 since 1968. Let's now ask a few questions.

Exercise A

1. *Does the value of your life - to yourself or to your loved ones - depend on the homicide or violent crime rate?* Or more accurately, is the value of your life a function of the homicide or violent crime rate, so that you hold your life more dear as the rate increases, and account your life less valuable as the rate decreases? No? Then,

2. Should the legal right to defend your life be function of the homicide or violate crime rate, so that the right comes into and goes out of existence as the rate rises or falls below a certain point? No? Then let me ask,

3. Is your resolve or willingness to defend your life a function of the homicide or violent crime rate, so that, if the rate is very low, you do not count your life worth fighting for and will not undertake great or serious efforts to protect it, but will do so if the homicide or violent crime rate becomes very high? No? Then let me ask,

4. Is the *means* you will permit yourself to use to defend yourself a function of the homicide or violent crime rate, so that if the rate is very low, you may use only whistles, or burglar and car alarms, cellular phones and your hands and feet to defend yourself, and as the rate becomes higher you may use chemical sprays, and if the rate becomes intolerable, well, then, you will perhaps believe that you may use a gun? And finally,

5. What rule of action does your habitual course of conduct reveal?

Perhaps you will think me obtuse for asking such manifestly absurd questions. I will tell you, however, that much of the gun-control debate in America presumes affirmative answers to these questions.

A few months ago, nationally syndicated columnist Charles Krauthammer published an article in the Washington Post (April 5, 1996) under the title, "Disarm the Citizenry. But Not Yet." There, he argued that Americans would never accept gun prohibition until government succeeded in decreasing the crime rate to acceptable levels. In other words, once the government proved to the citizens that it was good at controlling crime and had succeeded in reducing crime to very minimal levels, people would give up their guns. This leads us to ask,

Is the value of your life, and your willingness to use force if necessary to defend your life, a function of the effectiveness of government — so that, the better a job the police and the criminal justice system do, the less valuable you hold your life? No?

The handout includes various statistics regarding guns and crime. You may repeat the foregoing exercises at your leisure with any of these - or other - statistics. You may increase and decrease them as you like and ask yourself whether, at any level, they make a difference in your answers.

I suspect that in every case you will find an irreducible incongruity between the facts, as represented by the statistics, and a resolution that your life is worth defending and fighting for. Let me go further: I believe you may find that your resolution is not at all a function of such facts, that it is completely independent of these facts. In every case I think you will see that the questions commit the fundamental mistake, as Kierkegaard said, of endeavoring to quantify oneself into a qualitative decision.

Exercise B

1. If we believe that "ordinary citizens" as the Police Commissioner of New York likes to call us, should not resist crime, or fight back, but rely solely on police protection and

passive measures of resistance, like locks, avoidance, alarms, etc., then would it be permissible or appropriate to pass a law affirmatively prohibiting people from actively fighting back? Could government make it a crime to actively resist a criminal's demand, threat or violence?

Before you simply say, "Absurd!", consider that the state could justify such a law on the basis of public safety and order, as follows: if criminals know their victims will not resist, they will not need to use actual violence to get what they want, merely threaten it. If the state orders its citizens to cooperate when a criminal assault has been threatened, fewer people will be harmed, because the violence criminals use to establish dominance over their intended victims and coerce cooperation will not be necessary. So - could the government pass a law *ordering* intended victims to cooperate? If not, why not? The ever solicitous state is concerned *only* for your safety. Aren't you?

2. Is there a difference, in practical terms, between such a law and a law which prohibits citizens from using the most effective means of resisting violent crime?

Exercise C

Suppose such a law - compelling cooperation – were passed and it was one of the most effective laws ever made. All victims eagerly obeyed the law and readily cooperated, and no one was injured or physically harmed as a result. Query: knowing that the most certain way of avoiding physical injury and physical pain and suffering is to cooperate, should you, would you, readily accede to the criminal's demands?

Perhaps you will see where I am going with these questions. If your sole concern is with your physical safety, comfort and bodily integrity, and a statistical analysis of criminal assaults shows overwhelmingly that that result is most likely assured by cooperation — make the margin as large as you like, make it certain — then why not simply cooperate?

Often when we talk about the right of "self-defense" it appears to mean no more than this — the preservation of mere life or bodily integrity, the freedom from physical pain and suffering. Suppose a ready cooperation with criminal demands and threats best assured this result. Make it as probable as you like; make it certain. Assume that cooperation yields perfect self-defense: Now, should you cooperate? Or does this suggestion rankle or disturb you in some way? Why? Aren't you concerned foremost for your safety, your life?

Again, I apologize if these questions seem obtuse but, you know, much of the gun control debate in America proceeds implicitly on this basis. Police and government officials commonly recommend that victims should not fight back, particularly if it is *only* property that the criminal demands. Give the criminal what he wants, we are told. Don't provoke him, or make him angry, or give him a reason to hurt you.

Similarly, we are told we should not use guns to protect ourselves, because most times they will not help us - we won't be able to bring them into use quick enough. So of course because they do not provide perfect protection in all circumstances, and because we might have a wrong idea about the effectiveness of guns as talismans that magically ward off evil, we should not have them or use them at all.

(Interestingly, the same could be said about the police, right? They do not provide perfect protection; they may not be there to help you when you need them; relying on them as if they were talismans that warded off evil might get you in trouble; therefore don't rely on them, get rid of them. How curious that the same argument is never made about the police!)

Exercise D

Are the police the law? Are the police the law?

No, you say. We live under a government of laws, not of men, and this distinction is one of the crowning achievements of the human race. Much blood was shed to establish this principle, to learn this distinction.

I agree: the police are not the law. When they act, they either act in accordance with the law, or not, as does any man, the same as you or I.

We are often warned, in America, about the dangers of "taking the law into our own hands". Yet if we live under a government of laws and not of men, this is precisely what we all do - we all take the law into our own hands - in the sense that we either act in accordance with, and carry out the law - or not.

So - if the police are *not* the law, and if we are *not* the law, what is the basis for the privileged status of the police? Why are we told that we cannot do things that they can?

Exercise E

Is your life worth protecting? If so, whose responsibility is it to protect it?

If you believe that it is the police's, not only are you wrong - since the courts universally rule that they have no legal obligation to do so - but you face some difficult moral quandaries. How can you rightfully ask another human being to risk his life to protect yours, when you will assume no responsibility yourself? Because that is his job and we pay him to do it? Because your life is of incalculable value, but his is only worth the $30,000 salary we pay him? If you believe it reprehensible to possess the means and will to use lethal force to repel a criminal assault, how can you call upon another to do so for you?

Exercise F

We often claim to be shocked that violent criminals possess no respect for our property, our liberty or our lives. Yet why should criminals respect our lives or our liberty, when we ourselves do not value them highly enough to assume the responsibility to defend them, and do not hold them worth fighting for? Why, if society counsels a ready accession to the criminal's demands, why, if law enforcement itself counsels criminals that such cooperation is their due, why, if the criminal is not to be met with immediate, outraged resistance, would a criminal believe that what he is doing is *actually wrong*? Because laws make it so? Then his crime is solely against the state, not against the person of the victim.

Violent crime flourishes in good part because each of us refuses to condemn the violent criminal with our deeds at the precise moment that that condemnation is required, believing instead that laws will "communicate" —— and are sufficient to enforce —— values we are unwilling to battle for ourselves. We marvel that crimes that 30 years ago were unthinkable have become commonplace, never seeing that the increased depravity of criminals mirrors our own refusal to act upon moral judgment.

Closing

In closing, you will see that I did not speak too much about guns. That is because I believe that guns are only tools and that, ethically speaking, tools do not have moral effects. Their use depends entirely on our purpose and character.

In this regard let me tell you why I believe that guns are so reviled in our culture right now: Fundamentally, we do not value guns because we have rejected the responsibility that would make ownership and use of guns both necessary and meaningful. We have rejected the responsibility to defend our own lives and to assert our liberty, and have ceded that responsibility entirely to our government. Because we have rejected that responsibility, guns have only two remaining purposes: crime and sport. The interests of hobbyists and sportsmen will never trump the interest of the public in its own safety, so there is no end to restrictions on guns as a means of curbing crime.

I have two final observations to leave you with:

1. A people who will renounce the responsibility to defend their own lives — arguably the *most* fundamental of all responsibilities — and the right to possess and use the means necessary to fulfill that responsibility, have by that very act declared and proved themselves to be *irresponsible*, fundamentally irresponsible, and thereby *justify* their treatment by the government as *suspect*, as people whose worthiness and qualification for rights

and privileges must be tested and assured before granted by government.

2. If a people will renounce, and cede to their government the very responsibility to protect their own lives, and by extension, those of their loved ones, and the right to own and use the means necessary to fulfill that obligation, then there is *nothing, nothing,* that they will not cede to the government.

AGAINST PREVENTION

"To constitute a crime against human laws, there must be first a vicious will, and secondly, an unlawful act consequent upon such vicious will."

Sir William Blackstone,
Commentaries on the Laws of England

Who's Under Assault in the Assault Weapon Ban?

President Clinton suffered a stinging, embarrassing rebuke when 58 Democrats joined all but 11 Republicans and blocked release of the crime bill from committee to the floor of the House for a vote. One of its more controversial provisions, of course, is the ban on assault weapons. But the president and the Democratic leadership regrouped, offering compromise on "pork"projects and other items, and retaining the assault weapon ban significantly unchanged. Although many of the House Republicans and many of the 64 Democrats who voted against the bill did so largely because of the assault weapon ban, as Rep. Jack Brooks noted during Sunday's floor debate, "the people who hate guns are in the majority now."

While many Republicans worked hard to kill the assault weapon ban, few dared say so out loud and publicly confined their announced opposition to the bill to the excessive "pork" hidden in the guise of dubious social programs. This is a shame, for there are important reasons to oppose the assault weapon ban, reasons, moreover, that have nothing to do with guns or whether the ban will "work."

Supporters of the assault weapon ban have put forth essentially two reasons why these "weapons of war" should be prohibited. First, as Mr. Clinton has stated, they should be banned because they are the "weapons of choice of drug traffickers, gang members and paramilitary extremist groups."

Now, let's assume that the president is right, that assault weapons are indeed beloved by violent criminals, and that their rapid fire and large ammunition capacities make them eminently suitable for the evil designs of drug lords, gang members, lunatics and extremists. We still have one question. Are the rights and liberties that the law permits to the law-abiding dictated or determined by the choices and behavior of the lawless?

The essence of the "weapon of choice" argument is that, because criminals and madmen use these guns to commit crimes, the law-abiding must give them up. But to ban guns because criminals use them is to tell the innocent and law-abiding that their rights and liberties depend not on their own conduct, but on the conduct of the guilty and the lawless, and that the law will permit them to have only such rights and liberties as the lawless will allow.

By criminalizing an act that is not wrong in itself — the purchase and sale of a firearm — the ban violates the presumption of innocence, the principle that insures that government honors the liberty of its citizens until their deeds convict them. By completely banning the sale of assault weapons to prevent crime, the law effectively and irrebuttably presumes that all who want such a weapon are no better than murderers or madmen, forever ineligible to acquire these firearms.

Obviously, a law which restricts the liberty of the innocent because of the behavior of the guilty, that rests on the principle that the conduct of criminals dictates the scope of liberty that the law will allow to the rest of society, in no sense "fights" crime. It is, instead, a capitulation to crime, born of a society in full-bore retreat from crime, a society fearful of and desperately accommodating itself to crime.

A society that was, instead, outraged over crime, would boldly direct its energies against criminals, angrily resolved to surrender no ground, forfeit no liberties to the lawless. For society does not control crime, ever, by forcing the law-abiding to accommodate themselves to the expected behavior of criminals. Society controls crime by forcing criminals to accommodate themselves to the expected behavior of the law-abiding.

The "weapons of choice" justification of the ban is illegitimate, because it is unjust for the law to deprive the innocent of their liberties because of the behavior of the guilty. But supporters of the assault weapon ban have another, more powerful argument for why these weapons should be banned. Unlike the "weapon of choice" justification, this other argument does not depend on the fact that violent criminals like guns.

The second argument asserts that assault weapons should be banned because they are "weapons of war whose sole purpose is to kill people." No one, not even the law-abiding, has any legitimate reason to own a weapon that can fire so many rounds so quickly, suitable only for military purposes.

Recent legal and historical scholarship, such as Joyce Malcolm's new book, *To Keep and Bear Arms — The Origin of an Anglo-American Right* (Harvard University Press), is quite clear that the purpose of the Second Amendment was precisely to ensure that individuals had the right to keep and bear firearms suitable for militia use, for our nation was founded upon the belief that a citizen-militia was "necessary to the security of a free state."

The Second Amendment is a dead letter, however, in at least two of our branches of government. So let's set that aside. What's interesting about the "weapons of war" justification is — no one actually believes it.

Whatever sinister capabilities assault weapons have as compared to other firearms, whatever dark purpose spawned their creation, neither Congress, gun-control proponents nor the public claim that their ownership or use should be denied to the police or federal law enforcement agencies. Yet the nation's law enforcement officers are not warriors, hit men or death squads licensed to kill. Like law-abiding citizens, they may only use lethal force justifiably, in defense of themselves or others, or face the sanctions of criminal law.

How is it, then, that "assault weapons" magically transform into "counter-assault weapons" when handled by the police? And how do they revert to "deadly assault weapons" when handled by everyone else?

The fact that people believe that law enforcement may use these weapons demonstrates, of course, that people understand that the weapons have obvious and legitimate utility for defense of home, community and nation. This one fact shows that the guns are not evil of themselves, and do not whisper to their owners, taunting them to shoot children playing at recess or innocent bystanders in drive-by shootings.

This one fact shows that people understand that the responsible use of firearms depends first and foremost on the purpose and character of the person who wields the weapon. And because we know these things, this discrepancy between how we view ourselves and how we view the police holds the key to understanding what the assault weapon ban is really about.

A civilian who wants a weapon that looks and acts like a "weapon of war" is suspect. We fear his motives, his purity of heart. We do not fear the motives of the police or federal agents, because they are instituted and commissioned to protect us and our community. We do not fear "assault weapons" in the hands of the police because their mission is, as put by the Los Angeles Police Department's motto, "to protect and serve."

The support for the assault weapon ban thus reveals an awful truth: Our representatives, our president, and a sizable majority of Americans no longer believe or presume that their friends and neighbors — the many, common unknown people who make up their communities — act out of good and noble desire to defend themselves, their families and their communities from violent crime or civil disorder.

They will not trust their fellow, gun-owning Americans to act responsibly with firearms, because they do not perceive their fellow Americans to be harnessed or dedicated to the common good. No republic is established or long stands on such a foundation.

Polls show that about 70 percent of the American people support the assault weapon ban. This astonishing degree of support exists despite the fact that the L.A. riots demonstrated vividly and unassailably that a semiautomatic with large ammunition and rapid reload capacity is precisely the weapon a lone or small group of shopkeepers (and, by extension, a homeowner) needs to face down an angry mob.

It exists despite the fact that civilian firearms played a key role in maintaining law and order in southern Florida in the aftermath of Hurricane Andrew, when police and social services were disrupted and overwhelmed by the magnitude of the natural disaster.

The support exists despite the fact that ATF and FBI behavior at Waco should have taught us all to stop confusing the firearms proficiency and "professionalism" of law enforcement with sound and moral judgment. Yet the responsible use of firearms depends precisely on sound and moral judgment, and no republic is founded or stands upon the notion that the government possesses and exercises moral judgment superior to that of the people.

The facts prove powerless to derail the assault weapon ban because the law reflects, at bottom, our collective disavowal of any serious responsibility to protect ourselves or our communities from violent crime or civil disorder, and our belief that this responsibility, and the force necessary to execute that responsibility, lie exclusively in the domain of the state.

The common criticism that assault weapons have "no legitimate sporting purpose" thus expresses perfectly the view, now shared by more than two-thirds of our countrymen, that the American people are not fit for, nor to be trusted or burdened with, such weighty concerns or responsibilities as defense of home, community or country.

No, we wish to confine ourselves to, and are fit only for, our diversions, "bread and circuses." It is the responsibility of our more trustworthy servants in the government to take care of us, and we will do our part by complaining about their performance until they start doing a good job.

The assault weapon ban represents neither criminological nor moral progress, but irresponsibility, and lack of that faith and trust in our fellow man that is, at bottom, what we mean by community. The ban is wrong not only because it deprives the innocent of their liberty, but because it is a vote of no confidence in the character of the people.

While the great majority of Americans evidently no longer trust themselves or one another to behave responsibly with firearms intended for serious purposes, Congress errs if it abandons those who still recognize that self-government and the commitment to duty, honor and country require that each be prepared against the day when he must take up his arms, fully suitable to the purpose then at hand, and fight and risk life in defense of family, community or nation.

Failing that, all who support the ban should know this: When the president finally signs into a law a bill that includes an assault weapon ban, those who opposed that ban because of what the Founding Fathers intended for us, because of what we once were and what we should be, will know that their government regards them as criminals and that their countrymen renounce liberty at each turn for any promise of safety.

Fighting Crime by Creating Crime

Wwhat is the nature of gun control laws? What characteristic do they share, if any, despite the diversity of activities that they seek to regulate or prohibit? Let's review some modern federal gun control laws with an eye on this question.

Recent gun control began with the Gun Control Act of 1968. The civil rights movement was in full swing at the time. There had been several race riots and people feared there would be more. Groups like the Black Panthers were openly and notoriously brandishing shotguns and M-1 carbines. Ostensibly passed as a response to the political assassinations of the Kennedys and Martin Luther King, the act banned the interstate sale and shipment of rifles and other firearms through the mails — a mechanism, it was feared, that permitted easy, unregulated access to cheap, but deadly, surplus firearms for groups like the Panthers and Weathermen. Although many gun owners objected to this law, it can be fairly said that it was enacted in response — whether rational or not — to significant social and political upheavals in American society.

It is not so easy to point to such extraordinary events or such titanic forces for the gun control legislation that would follow. Yet with subsequent legislation it would become ever more clear that gun control had become a cultural crusade. Somehow, through the turbulent '60s, the gun had become the symbol for all that was despicable and low in the American character, all that had to be eradicated.

No major federal gun control legislation was enacted during the 16-year period that followed the GCA, 1969 to 1985. In 1986, the McClure-Volkmer Bill, also known as the Firearms Owners Protection Act (FOPA), eased some of the restrictions imposed by the GCA to make it easier to purchase and transport firearms across state lines. The act also made it unlawful to transfer a firearm, to sell or dispose of any firearm or ammunition to illegal aliens, persons dishonorably discharged from the armed forces, and persons who had renounced their U.S. citizenship. FOPA is generally best remembered, however, for making it unlawful for any person to possess or transfer a machine-gun that was not lawfully possessed before the date of FOPA's enactment. That is, FOPA basically prohibited the purchase or ownership of machine guns manufactured after the date of enactment.

As their was no outbreak of machine-gun violence in 1986, the motivation for this prohibition apparently sprang from the self-evident truth that there is no good reason why citizens should be permitted to own machine-guns. If its name was any indicator, the law thus "protected" firearms owners by preventing them from acting upon an obviously incorrect belief about this matter.

The Undetectable Firearms Act of 1988, inspired by a so-called "terrorist pistol," the Glock, was enacted to outlaw those weapons that were not detectable by airport metal detectors, and mandated that handguns have a certain minimum metal content. The law expires in 2003 unless re-enacted.

Possession of firearms and other dangerous weapons in "federal facilities" was also outlawed in 1988. This law consoles the widows, widowers and orphaned children of the numerous employees of the postal service who have been murdered by fellow workers with the knowledge that, although the law deprived their husbands or wives, mothers and fathers of the ability to defend themselves, their murderers can be tagged with *federal* murder charges in lieu of, or addition to already applicable *state* murder charges. This trade-off was evidently considered a good bargain by our representatives, senators and president.

The Gun-Free School Zone Act of 1990 made it unlawful for a person to possess a firearm in a place that the person knows or has reason to believe is a "school zone," defined as the school grounds and the area 1000 feet in all directions from the school grounds. (The law did not apply to firearms on private property within the school zone; residents who lived near schools were not immediately reclassified as criminals.)

The logic of this law is flawless and unassailable. Schools are hallowed places for learning, and no one can effectively learn if they are worried about guns and violence, if they see their friends shot down, or if people are constantly diving for cover. Ergo, schools must be gun-free zones. Since this logic can be applied practically everywhere, it is a sign of the insincere half-heartedness with which our legislators attempt (pretend?) to solve society's problems that they did not boldly declare all places (except, perhaps, target shooting ranges) gun-free zones.

It is impossible to be productive and do a good job at work if one is constantly distracted by the thought that there may be guns in the workplace, and that lethal violence may erupt. Ergo, all workplaces must be gun-free zones. It is impossible to get a good night's sleep if one is worried that the bullets will soon start flying. Ergo, bedrooms, and all areas within 1000 feet of bedrooms, should be gun-free zones. And so on. Lacking the courage to follow their logic to its conclusion, our legislators missed an important chance to make all of our zones a much safer place. In fact, it would have been easier to simply declare that each individual is a bullet-free zone.

The year 1993 gave us two important acts — the Brady Act and the Federal Firearms License Reform Act. By imposing a national five business day waiting period for a handgun purchases, the Brady Act imposed a prior restraint upon the exercise of a fundamental individual right (that is, if one labors under the belief that the Second Amendment protects a fundamental individual right to own firearms). Brady effectively presumes that handgun purchasers are "guilty" — unauthorized to own a handgun — until proven innocent by an absence of damning records among the federal and state files.

The 1993 License Reform Act increased the first-time license fees for firearms dealers from $25 to $200, and the renewal fee from $25 to $90, required that the dealer conduct his business from fixed premises (no more operating out of car trunks in the inner cities!) and certify that the use of those premises was authorized under state and local law, including zoning ordinances. These changes were enacted to significantly eliminate the number of persons obtaining FFLs and are accomplishing that goal.[1] The 1993 licensing act also eliminated firearms dealers' and manufacturers' Fourth Amendment rights to be free from unreasonable searches and seizures. The BATF "may inspect or examine the inventory and records of a licensed importer, licensed manufacturer or licensed dealer *without such reasonable cause or warrant*" [emphasis added] to ensure compliance with federal record keeping requirements. Persons who sell or make firearms are evidently second class citizens who do not deserve Fourth Amendment rights — doubtless because they are merchants of death.

The year 1994 gave us the "Public Safety and Recreational Firearms Use Protection Act," more commonly known as the "assault weapons ban." That act enhances the public's safety by banning possession and sale of semi-automatic firearms manufactured after September 13, 1994 that have two or more military accoutrements such as pistol grips, bayonet lugs, folding stocks or flash suppressors. Since the act did not ban semi-automatic

---

1 Since enactment through mid-1999, the number of licensed firearms dealers has declined approximately 67 percent, from about 250,000 to about 80,000.

weapons with the same performance capabilities that lack the military accoutrements, the act might have been better named, "The Illusion of Public Safety and Recreational Firearms Use Protection Act." Alas, the federal government is not subject to truth in advertising laws.

The assault weapon ban also "protected" the recreational use of firearms by providing that the hunting and sporting rifles and shotguns designated on an attached list — some 670 firearms — were not "assault weapons." Thus, no one had to worry that their favorite hunting rifles or shotguns would be classified in BATF regulations as illegal assault weapons.

Finally, the act banned possession and sale of magazines capable of holding more than 10 rounds that are manufactured after September 13, 1994. The assault weapon and magazine prohibitions will expire in 2004 unless re-enacted.

Last in our survey, the 1994 federal crime act made it unlawful to sell a firearm or ammunition to any person the seller knows or has reason to believe is subject to a court order restraining the person from "harassing, stalking, or threatening an intimate partner," or for any such person to possess a firearm.

This by no means details all of the federal gun laws since 1968, but is perhaps enough of a survey to examine the nature of such laws. Now certainly it may be argued that the problem with all of these laws is that they infringe the right to keep and bear arms by imposing a prior restraint on the exercise of that right, and therefore deserve to be struck down as violations of the Second Amendment.

But there is another perspective from which it may be said that the problem with these laws has *nothing* to do with guns. In this view, the gun laws are only a part of a more general class of laws that all share a certain fundamental characteristic, that all spring from a common purpose and desire. If we truly wish to end legislation like Brady, we must grasp the underlying impulse from which this legislation springs. Unless we understand and reject that impulse, and the principle behind this *type* of legislation, the impulse will remain the well-spring for a thousand new laws.

The federal gun control laws since at least 1968 all share the following fundamental characteristic: *they outlaw or restrict an activity that is not inherently wrong in order to prevent harm.* Stated simply, the laws create crimes in order to *stop* crimes; they create a new class of criminals in order to eliminate, or at least decrease the size or dangerousness of, another class of criminals.

The common law distinguished between crimes that were *malum in se*, or morally wrong in themselves, like rape, murder or robbery, and crimes that were *malum prohibitum*, wrong because prohibited by a legislative pronouncement. There is nothing inherently wrong, or evil, with purchasing a firearm across state lines, entering a post office while carrying a firearm, purchasing a firearm without first enduring a background check, or owning an "assault weapon" or magazines capable of holding more than ten rounds. These activities in and of themselves harm no one; the deed in itself is not immoral.

And so that there's no quibbling here, let's be clear about this. Ethically speaking, there is in fact no harm in a convicted felon purchasing a firearm, regardless of whether at that moment he plans to use the firearm in the commission of a crime. The act of acquiring and owning the firearm in fact harms no one, and until the very moment he commits his crime, the felon is free, like each of us, to choose good over evil, and reverse course.

The purchase of a handgun across state lines, or without a background check, has been made, however, *malum prohibitum*, declared wrong, as a means of preventing the wrong people from obtaining firearms, or keeping firearms out of certain places, to *prevent* harm. Otherwise law-abiding citizens, such as firearm dealers, are now subject to the risk of becoming criminals, not because *their* conduct or activity harms any one, but solely to prevent *other* persons from becoming criminals or perpetrating criminal misdeeds.

Yes, the concept of prevention sounds appealing. Why *wait* only to punish people *after* the fact, when the murder, the rape, has already been committed, and it is *too late*? What could possibly be wrong with preventing persons from selling firearms to convicted felons? Why should society knowingly take a risk that convicted felons *might* have reformed? What could possibly be wrong with taking steps to stop crime *before* it occurs, with saving lives?

Perhaps the pursuit of safety through prevention seems reasonable, even though one perhaps recognizes that there is a certain madness in the notion of creating new crimes to eliminate (more serious) crimes, in restricting liberty to purchase safety. Perhaps we believe, as Sarah Brady likes to say, that "if it saves even one life, it is worth it." Well, then, if we propose to make this bargain, let us look squarely at what it means to criminalize otherwise innocent activities as a means of preventing crime.

First, recognize that only laws that criminalize behavior *malum in se* and impose restrictions on liberty (punishment) *after the fact*, when it is *too late*, accord with the presumption of innocence, the principle that government honors the liberty of its citizens until their deeds convict them. Laws that criminalize innocent behavior in order to prevent crimes effectively presume guilt. *Brady*, for example, in seeking to *prevent* harm, effectively presumes that all handgun purchasers are madmen or felons, and all firearm dealers are engaged in criminally abetting the commission of a crime with a firearm, unless the purchaser's innocence, i.e., his eligibility to acquire the gun, is proven by an absence of damning records in the hands of the authorities.

Second, laws that criminalize conduct not wrong in itself to prevent crime make the behavior of criminals the measure of the rights and scope of liberty that the law will permit to the innocent. Assault weapons are dangerous in the hands of criminals; therefore, no one shall have them. Such laws tell the innocent and law-abiding that their rights and liberties depend not on their own conduct, but on the conduct of the lawless, that the law will permit the innocent to have only such rights and liberties as criminals will allow.

73

A law which restricts the liberty of the innocent because of the behavior of the guilty, that rests on the principle that the conduct of criminals dictates the scope of liberty the law will allow to the rest of society, in no sense "fights" crime. For society has permitted its fear of crime, and craving for safety, to turn the force of law against the innocent and law-abiding. Far from *fighting* crime, the criminalization of otherwise innocent activities represents a society in *retreat* before crime. This is society desperately accommodating itself to crime.

Third, laws that criminalize innocent behavior in order to prevent harm make a mockery of, and trivialize, laws that criminalize behavior that is truly wrong. Guns are banned in post offices and school zones. Why this partiality to post offices and schools? Are we protecting hallowed places from being defiled, or lives? Are there some places where it is acceptable to murder or threaten others with firearms? The selectivity in the law is inherently unsupportable, so that it is apparent that the law is merely a political, manipulative ploy, or is purely symbolic. What do such laws say? That murder is wrong, but it is really, really wrong, and we really, really mean it, in schools and post offices? In its implicit suggestion that murder is more wrong in some places than others and will be subject to more punishment if committed in some places than others, the law undermines the seriousness of murder, reveals, in fact, that we do not take *mere murder* seriously. Faced with the dire fact of violent crime, we retreat into symbolism.

Yet to one who believes that by relinquishing a little liberty, and bearing some slight inconveniences, we might truly purchase greater safety, the foregoing may be regarded as so much libertarian gibberish, and less than convincing. Yes, a rigid adherence to the presumption of innocence grants maximum scope to individual liberty. But, the criticism might run, too much emphasis has been, is placed on individual freedom.

We do not live alone, but in society, and the actions of some members, such as gun dealers, regardless of whether they are evil or wrong in themselves, have consequences that adversely affect others. There is no reason that some persons in a good position to thwart criminal endeavors should not be compelled to join in the fight against crime, to prevent crime and thus make our society a safer place.

The problem with this "interconnectedness of all things" argument is that it has no logical or natural stopping place: it can be used to justify absolutely anything, any excess. Once the principle of punishing only activities that are actually wrong is abandoned, we have no star to guide us.

Consider. Our society generally believes that drug use for pleasure (rather than as medicine) is wrong. To *prevent* this, we have completely banned the purchase and sale of certain psychotropic drugs. Alas, this was not sufficient; drug use continues at unacceptable levels. Accordingly, bankers, car dealers and anyone who receives payment in cash exceeding $10,000 must report the fact to the authorities, so that the authorities may trace drug money laundering activities. Landlords who rent property where drug dealing occurs risk loss of their property to the government, for not preventing what the government could not; they should know what happens on their premises and take action to evict the dealers.

Oh, but why stop here? Surely the grocery store managers in drug infested neighborhoods know who the drug dealers and users are. Why not prohibit them from selling food to these scum? Are we serious about ostracizing these people and condemning their behavior or not? The interconnectedness of all things argument has no objection to it; it contains no principle that would say, thus far, and no further! Why just landlords and bankers and not grocery store clerks? Aren't they all part of the great drug dealer chain of being?

And have our prevention efforts abated drug use? Is the world, in fact, a better and safer place — or have we merely succeeded in moving the battleground to a new location? Alas, prohibition was not quite the success we all hoped for. Landlords and bankers must now be conscripted in the good fight; the Feds must follow the activity in our bank accounts. The circle has expanded to include more persons involved in the great drug dealer chain of being.

So here let us note the fourth characteristic of laws that criminalize innocent conduct in order to prevent crime before it occurs. To the extent that they "work," they do not so much actually prevent the crime they aim at, as locate the battleground for our next prevention efforts. Each prevention effort is, thus, "a good first step." The problem is that each step is *only* a first step: the goal endlessly recedes before us.

This is easy to see with gun control legislation. Brady prevents criminals from buying guns from legitimate dealers. Next we must shut down unregulated sales at flea markets and gun shows, and require homeowners to keep their guns in vaults, so that criminals cannot obtain their guns from any conceivable source.

Once these efforts have succeeded, so that the gun market for criminals is converted into an illegal, underground market like the market for illegal drugs, we will need tight import restrictions to shut down the borders. Eventually, we will need to regulate sales of metal-working tools by Sears, and implicate everyone in the great gun dealer chain of being.

By now it should be evident what the project of all laws that criminalize innocent conduct in order to prevent crime is: to so arrange the material conditions of life that those disposed to act upon their evil intentions will have no means of realizing their designs. Matters must be so arranged that, though criminals will want to use guns, they just won't be able to get them. People will want drugs, they just won't be able to buy them. Crazy people will want to blow up buildings; they just won't be able to. Thus will the world be made a safer place.

And now we come to the critical point, the self-destructive contradiction inherent in laws that criminalize innocent conduct to prevent crime before it occurs: *their goal is to make responsibility irrelevant.* It doesn't matter if criminals *want* to commit murder with guns; we will arrange things so that they simply *cannot.* Pass Brady and a few other well-crafted laws, vigorously enforce them, and it won't *matter* whether people act responsibly or not. Their irresponsible intentions will be rendered impotent and irrelevant.

Query: how does the law have the moral authority to hold people responsible for their behavior, if the law is engaged in a project whose operative presumption is that responsibility and irresponsibility can be made irrelevant, and are a matter of indifference? How do criminals, how does *anyone*, learn that they are responsible for their actions, if the law is engaged in a mighty project to render it irrelevant whether one does or does not want to act responsibly?

And if we think that laws designed to prevent crime can indeed make the world a safer place, we should ask ourselves this: How, exactly, is the world made a safer place by making self-control and responsibility irrelevant?

Guns and Schools

A short time ago, I reviewed federal gun control legislation since 1968, including the Gun-Free School Zone Act of 1990. This law was struck down in 1996 by the Supreme Court on the ground that the Congress of the United States did not have authority under the interstate commerce clause (Article I, Section 8, clause 3, U.S. Constitution) to pass such a law. The Court noted that regulating the presence of guns in schools was not a "commercial" activity. Congress has no general power under the Constitution to enact laws regulating health, education, crime and welfare: those powers are reserved to the states under the Tenth Amendment. Since the law did not fall within the commerce clause, it was unconstitutional.

Not to be thwarted, Congress reenacted the Gun Free School Zone Act as part of its final budget resolutions before the November 1996 elections. This time, Congress included "findings" as part of the law explaining why guns in schools have a deleterious effect on interstate commerce and made the law apply only to guns which have, or which consist of materials which have, moved in interstate commerce. Congress thus means to test the limits of its authority with the Supreme Court. Obviously, if the

Court accepts this as sufficient basis for upholding the law, there is no law that Congress cannot pass by the simple expedient of including "findings" on how the regulated activity affects commerce. That is, Congress will have no limit on its authority except the Bill of Rights.

A reader of that earlier essay wrote to take me to task for a statement I made about the Gun Free School Zone Act of 1990. My words, he thought, gave support to our enemies. Since this law has now been reenacted, it is worthwhile to revisit this issue.

The law makes it a crime to possess a gun in a "school zone," defined as the school grounds and the area 1,000 feet in radius around those grounds. Here is what I said:

> "The logic of this law is flawless and unassailable. Schools are hallowed places for learning, and no one can effectively learn if they are worried about guns and violence, if they see their friends shot down, or if people are constantly diving for cover. Ergo, schools must be gun-free zones.
>
> Since this logic can be applied practically everywhere, it is a sign of the insincere half-heartedness with which our legislators attempt (pretend?) to solve society's problems that they did not boldly declare all places (except, perhaps, target shooting ranges) gun-free zones."

My critic did not like this. Here was a gun magazine, representing gun owners, actually saying that the logic of the gun free school zone act was "flawless," and that the only problem with the law was that it did not go far enough!

Well, my critic has a point, but only to a point. I stand by my prior statement, and I will now use it to make a new argument: The reason we have laws like the gun-free school zone act is that our politicians know that the overwhelming majority of the American electorate reacts to laws solely on an emotional level. "Of course there shouldn't be guns in schools!" That sentiment is the rock-hard foundation for the gun-free school zone act.

There is nothing, nothing that anyone can say about guns in schools that will change that sentiment, not that the problem has been highly exaggerated, and not that we already have laws that prevent such a thing. Trying this tack will only get one branded as an "extremist" who thinks that maybe guns in schools are a good idea. There is only one antidote to this lunacy and that is: actually thinking about what the law means.

When I say "thinking," I mean, identifying the operating principle at work, and testing its validity by pursuing it to its logical conclusion. Obviously, the motivating principle of the gun-free school zone act is the presumption that laws can keep guns out of schools.

But unlike the laws against rape, robbery, murder or assault, the law does not assign a punishment for wrong behavior after the fact; instead, the school-zone act seeks to prevent harm by banning the instrumentality of the crime. Its unspoken premise is that *the law has the power to prevent crime.*

Now if this is what our Congresspersons really believe, then why stop with schools? Don't we all deserve to live, and to be protected from violence? What about hospitals, restaurants, our homes, for God's sake? If laws can really prevent crime, then why be so circumspect? Why not declare all individuals bullet-free zones and make our country a safer place?

But, you say, a law that declared individuals bullet-free zones would be absurd. Obviously a law cannot actually make a person "bullet-free." Yes, but it is no more absurd than the gun-free school zone act, for neither can any law make a school "gun-free." By universalizing the operating principle of that law, and extending its supposed benefits to everyone, I have merely made its absurdity apparent.

That a person believes the gun-free school zone act to be a "rational" law or a "good idea" merely reflects his failure to understand the absurdity of the law's founding principle. Its seeming "good idea" quality stems solely from an emotional reaction to guns in schools that derives ultimately from a natural desire to secure the safety of our children.

No law has the power to prevent crime. Laws that pretend otherwise make a mockery of law. How so? In order for the gun-free school zone act to "work," we must expect that a person who is willing to commit a robbery, rape, murder or assault will be prevented because, while the laws proscribing punishment for *those* crimes have no hold upon him, he will have nothing but the utmost respect for the rule about not bringing guns to school.

Ever wonder why all gun control laws exhibit this absurdity? It is because these laws are founded on the monumental presumption that laws control conduct, i.e., that we are not free.

A person obeys a law either because he *respects* the law (whether because he approves the moral judgement embodied in the law, because laws represent the consensus of his fellow citizens whose good will he values, or from sheer loyalty to the rule of law) or because he *fears* the consequences of breaking the law. In either case, *the person restrains himself;* the control exerted by law rests, irretrievably, upon *self-control,* that is, upon a man's own sense of responsibility. Without that self-control, without that sense of responsibility, the law has no force but brute force.

God made man free; he *is* free. No power on earth can change that fact. When once a man chooses to disdain the consequences, no law can stop him — whether his decision be to march boldly into Tiannamen Square to stand in front of the advancing tanks, and expose the law and his government for what it is, or to rape, rob, or murder.

Because God made man free, *all legal restraint rests upon self-restraint; all legal control rests upon self-control.* Laws that only punish conduct that is morally wrong after the fact (like the laws proscribing murder) acknowledge this moral reality. Laws that pretend to stop crime before it occurs by prohibiting conduct that is not morally wrong, like gun-control laws, make a mockery of law. How? Because they presume that, by arranging external reality (e.g., by banning guns in schools, or anywhere else), we can eliminate man's freedom, and as a result, his irresponsible behavior.

Don't see it? Here is the theory of how the gun-free school zone act will work: If there are no guns in schools, the kids won't be able to shoot one another, even if they *want* to. By banning guns, we can make it *irrelevant* whether the kids can control themselves. They don't *have* to be good, or responsible; by creating a safe (i.e., gun-free) environment for them, we control the kids. Thus, the rubric of the gun-free school zone act is: by eliminating freedom, we eliminate the need for responsible behavior. The problem is, such a law can never "work," because freedom *cannot* be eliminated, and without responsibility, law has no force but brute force.

Well, it is doubtful that our legislators actually believe that the law will keep guns out of schools, or that laws can actually prevent crime. No, they're simply pandering to the never-ending demands of the electorate for "safety". And so, unfortunately, the real lesson of the gun-free school zone act is this: law in America has become a psy-op —— a tool for satisfying emotional needs. And the majesty of our Constitution has been reduced to the care and feeding of emotional two-year olds.

TEACH YOUR CHILDREN WELL

In Alexandria, Louisiana, 8-year old honor student Kameryan Lueng was suspended from school when she brought her grandfather's engraved gold pocket watch to school for show-and-tell. The watch was on a chain which was attached to a one-inch knife. She was required to spend one month at the Redirection Academy, a school for problem students, before being allowed to return. Her mother, Cheryl Lueng, reports that "Kameryan cried when I told her she couldn't go back to her school Monday. She knows she broke a rule, but now she feels like a criminal."

In Kingwood, Texas, 13 year old Brooke Olson was suspended for a day for carrying a bottle of Advil in her backpack instead of giving it to the school nurse. In Fairborn, Ohio, 13 year old Erica Taylor was suspended for 9 days for carrying Midol. She fared better, however, than Kimberly Smart, 14, who was suspended for 14 days because she gave Erica the Midol. The school reasoned that distributing the drugs was a more serious offense than simply having them!

These stories, and others like them, are told in a March 12, 1997 New York Times article describing the mandatory punishment of students under "zero tolerance" policies for drugs and weapons in the nation's schools ("School Codes Without Mercy Snare Pupils Without Malice", p. A1). Pressure for adopting the policies comes from a number of sources.

The Federal Gun-Free School Zone Act of 1994 requires states that receive federal funds for elementary and secondary education to expel any student caught carrying a gun to school for one year. President Clinton urged schools to adopt zero tolerance policies for guns and drugs in his 1997 State of the Union address. The American Federation of Teachers actively lobbies for state laws requiring schools to adopt zero tolerance policies. School boards adopt the policies thinking they will create safe environments for children, to reassure worried parents and, in the words of Robert Nash, a spokesman for the Texas Federation of Teachers, to send "a message to students that we mean business, that their actions will have consequences."

The *Times* reports that as the use of these policies spreads, "there is growing debate about whether mandatory punishment makes sense in cases like Kameryan's or other incidents . . . in which there was no intent to cause harm." Other educators, however, "say the benefit of zero-tolerance policies in raising a school's overall standard of conduct outweighs any harm done to any child who inadvertently breaks a rule."

Here is a fresh illustration of what passes for moral judgment in latter-day America. A policy is "good," and to be recommended, if the anticipated benefits will exceed the expected costs; the policy is "bad" if the reverse is true. The question whether any particular individual acts rightly or wrongly, judged by a moral standard, has disappeared; the question whether it is right or wrong to punish a particular person, judged by a moral standard, has disappeared.

In other words, morality itself has disappeared. The only question is whether a "policy" is likely to produce the positive benefits that we all want. Morality is chucked for the sake of satisfying the demand, "Just give us what we want!"

While the eager practitioners of this philosophy generally are unaware of it, the essence of their utilitarian pursuit of the "greatest good for the greatest number" is the belief that civilization depends on human sacrifice. Lest you think this mere rhetoric, consider. Absolutely no one believes that Kameryan Lueng intended to harm anyone. Nor does anyone claim that she acted recklessly, endangering others. Despite the innocence of her intentions and the safety of her conduct, however, she is punished, and treated no differently than if she had brought a knife to school to murder. Having done no wrong, morally speaking, an eight-year old girl is punished to serve as an example to others, while the authorities, and possibly society at large, count the undeserved harm to her as a small price to pay in their quest to secure the greater good.

Yet the implications of the utilitarian justification for zero tolerance policies do not begin to tell the real story why such policies are an abomination. To understand that, it is first necessary to comprehend what it is that makes an act right or wrong.

For at least the last two thousand years, religious authorities and moral philosophers have argued that it is the individual's *intent* that makes an action good or evil, praiseworthy or blameworthy. No action, taken by itself and abstracted from the intent that motivated the action, may be judged either good or bad. It is what is in one's heart that matters.

For example, in both murder and killing in self-defense, the action is the same (force or violence is used) and the result is the same (a person is killed). What distinguishes the rightness of the one from the wrongness of the other, in constitutive part, is the intent with which the act was done.

In one case, a person acts defensively to stop aggression and preserve life — the defender's own, or that of others. This act is called self-defense, is justified in the eyes of the law, and praiseworthy among general society. In the other, a person acts with intent to kill out of anger, frustration, hatred, or otherwise for no justifiable reason. This act is termed murder, is punishable at law, and roundly condemned as evil by all society.

Fundamental to the common law developed by our English ancestors was the notion that, for an act to be criminal, and therefore deserving of blame and punishment, the act had to be accompanied by bad intent — either a willful intent to harm, or a reckless disregard of the consequences of one's actions. It has been the great innovation of modern law to do away with this requirement.

Innumerable criminal laws on the books no longer require that the person committing the "crime" have actually harmed anyone or intended to harm anyone. Virtually all federal gun control laws fall into this category. Consider, for example, the "crime" of selling a handgun to a non-resident, or the "crime" of carrying a large folding knife in one's pocket into a post office while mailing a letter.

"Zero tolerance" policies against drugs and weapons in schools are but another example of such laws. Criminal or bad intent is not required, as the case of Kameryan Lueng plainly shows. An eight year old girl thought she would please her teacher and entertain her classmates by showing them an ornate and unusual old watch. She was rewarded with ostracism and censure, treated as a common criminal, and sent to be "re-educated" with juvenile delinquents.

Ah, the humanity. What fine people we all are. How choice — if, for once, getting tough on crime meant getting tough on actual criminals, that is, people who have *actually done something morally wrong*! Apparently this is beyond us, though, for we are all so very, very busy posturing and "sending messages."

Since intent is the essence of whether an act is moral or immoral, a law that ignores intent ignores moral content, ignores morality itself. Such a law proclaims that the moral content of your actions or your character is *irrelevant*. Such laws proclaim that the society in which you live does not care if you acted morally or not; it just wants you to follow orders, and is only interested in your capacity to follow orders.

Now if the essence of man's dignity is his capacity for moral judgment, his capacity to know and choose between good and evil, and to act accordingly, then laws that ignore intent declare man's moral nature irrelevant, and so express the most profound contempt for one's fellow man.

One sees this quite clearly in the treatment of students like Kameryan Lueng under zero tolerance policies. We simply cannot be bothered to decide whether Kameryan actually did anything wrong, that is, to make an actual judgment about the rectitude of her conduct. We think and care so little of her, we count the moral content of her action and her exercise of responsibility so meaningless, we regard her character as so immaterial, that she is condemned despite her innocence and freely sacrificed to the "policy" and the greater good it promises, for the sake of the results we so desperately crave.

Like all laws that do not require criminal intent, zero tolerance policies *dismiss* man's moral nature. Such laws, therefore, do indeed "send a message" and teach a profound lesson to students like Kameryan Lueng: moral character is irrelevant, acting on the basis of your understanding of right and wrong does not matter to your fellow citizens, and will not be respected by your government. All that matters is your capacity to follow orders, however far those orders be divorced from morality.

Schools are often criticized these days for failing to teach the simple basics of reading, English, math and history. In their quick embrace of policies that teach and encourage mindless, rigorous compliance with soulless orders, however, they are indeed preparing their students for life in the kind of world to come.

AGAINST UTILITY

"As soon as the will begins to cast a covetous eye on the outcome, the individual begins to become immoral —— the energy of the will becomes torpid, or it develops abnormally into an unhealthy, unethical, mercenary hankering that, even if it achieves something great, does not achieve it ethically —— the individual demands something other than the ethical itself."

Soren Kierkegaard,
*Concluding Unscientific Postscript to
Philosophical Fragments*

You're Doing This Because of the Numbers?

Should your personal decision whether to own or use a gun be based on, or justified by, the results of a rigorous statistical analysis of whether the benefits of gun ownership and use outweigh the costs of gun ownership and misuse? That is the underlying assumption of the cover story of the August 15, 1994 issue of *U.S. News and World Report*, "Should You Own a Gun?."

Once you sweep away anecdotal stories of this or that particular case of accidental death, suicide, murder or successful self-defense, *U.S. News* avers, "the quarrel over guns for self-defense boils down to the seminal researchers on the subject . . .": Florida State University criminology professor Gary Kleck and Director of the Center for Injury Control at Emory University, Dr. Arthur Kellerman.

The article then devotes considerable coverage to the apparently conflicting findings of these two men. Kleck's latest findings, based on his own 1993 random survey of approximately 5,000 households, are that guns are used in self-defense up to 2.4 million times a year.

Since Bureau of Justice Statistics estimate that approximately 1.1 million violent crimes were committed with guns in 1992,

Kleck's research suggests that guns are used far more often to deter than to commit crime.

Even more astounding, 1 in 6 of Kleck's respondents who had used a gun in self defense was almost certain that a life would have been lost without the gun, implying that guns save about 400,000 lives each year. Kleck points out that even if only one-tenth of those people were right, the number of lives saved by guns would still exceed the 38,000 annually killed by guns.

The *U.S. News* article also reports Kleck's contention that people who defend themselves with a gun are *more* likely to successfully resist the crime and *less* likely to be hurt. His analysis of National Crime Survey data for 1979-1987 showed that criminals were successful in only 14% of burglaries at occupied residences whose owners defended their property with guns, as compared to a success rate of 33% overall.

In addition, a new Bureau of Justice survey indicates that only 20% of crime victims who defended themselves with a firearm suffered injury, while twice that many (40%) were injured when they defended themselves with another weapon.

Critics who disagree with Kleck generally cite the Census Bureau's annual National Crime Victimization Survey, which indicates that only about 80,000, not 2.4 million, crime victims per year use firearms to defend themselves. If that number is right, criminal use of firearms would outnumber the use of guns in self-defense by about 14 to 1, suggesting that guns are far more of a menace than a boon to society.

But Kleck claims that the survey is a poor measure of the use of guns in self-defense because it is not anonymous and is conducted by government (Census Bureau) agents, who visit the same household seven times over a three-year period. In these circumstances, Kleck believes, respondents are unlikely to talk freely about defensive uses of guns involving domestic violence or rape, or cases where they were illegally carrying firearms in public, resulting in understated findings.

While Kleck's statistics appear to vindicate gun ownership, Kellerman's statistics appear to vindicate gun prohibition. Kellerman is known for three studies which appeared in *The New England Journal of Medicine*, two of which received prominent newspaper coverage.

In the first study, Kellerman reviewed six years of gunshot deaths in Seattle, and found that for every case of a self-protection homicide in the home, there were 1.3 accidental deaths, 4.6 criminal homicides and 37 suicides. Kellerman thus concluded that guns in the home were 43 times more likely to kill a family member or acquaintance than an intruder, suggesting that it is criminally irresponsible to keep a gun in the home for self-defense.

In his latest study, Kellerman studied homicides in the home in Memphis, Cleveland and Seattle over a five year period, and compared households in which homicides took place to households containing demographically similar victims but in which no homicide took place. The goal of the comparison was to identify the factors affecting a family's risk of a homicide in the home. Kellerman found that homes containing guns were almost three times more likely to be the scene of a homicide than comparable homes without guns. Kellerman believes his studies strongly show that "the risks of having a gun in the home substantially outweigh the benefits," and that "people should be strongly discouraged from keeping guns in their homes."

The goal of Kellerman's researches is to establish that guns cause violence or homicide in the way that smoking causes lung cancer and heart disease. The gun is a kind of agent, like a chemical or microbe, that acts on the owner, leading him to commit crimes that he would otherwise not commit.

The gun owner's character or "morality" becomes irrelevant to determining whether he will use guns responsibly, just as character or morality is irrelevant to whether you will get lung cancer if you smoke. If research could establish this type of connection between guns and homicide or violence then, presumably, society would be justified in banning or severely controlling guns, just as it might ban or regulate smoking, or require vaccination to prevent smallpox or tuberculosis.

Kellerman's critics, however, contend that his results are highly and erroneously skewed because he uses death as the sole criterion for measuring the risks and benefits of gun ownership, and thereby ignores the fact that in about 99% of defensive uses of firearms, no one is killed. By ignoring this huge body of successful self-defense with firearms that does not result in death, his studies are incomplete cost-benefit analyses, because they almost exclusively measure only the costs of gun ownership and use.

Critics further charge that while Kellerman's findings establish a strong correlation between guns and homicide, they do not prove that guns *cause* violence that would otherwise not occur. It may be that the people committing homicides with guns are violent people for whom preying on family, acquaintances and strangers is a way of life, and their ownership and use of guns is an extension of their desire to perpetrate their violence. That is, it may not be the guns that cause violence, but that persons of violent temper naturally desire to and do own guns, and use them in their predatory activities. Eliminating the guns, therefore, would not necessarily eliminate or lessen the violence.

Having presented the findings of these prominent social scientists pro and con, the *U.S. News* article leaves us to judge for ourselves whether it is better to own a firearm for self-defense, in the hope that we will judge rationally based on the best information available.

The assumption at work here is that if you believe Kleck's findings, or believe that the benefits of gun ownership that his research discloses outweigh the costs disclosed by Kellerman, your are justified in your decision to own or carry a gun. If, however, you believe Kellerman's findings, or believe that the costs his research discloses outweigh the benefits disclosed by Kleck, you are justified in your decision to not own or carry a gun, and to work to ban or restrict gun ownership.

Both approaches to decision-making are, however, equally wrong.

Kellerman's statistics do not prove that guns cause crime. But neither do Kleck's statistics prove that guns provide protection. Kellerman's statistics, even if faultless, provide no justification for a decision to not own or use a gun. But neither do Kleck's statistics provide a justification for owning or carrying a gun.

Admittedly, this sounds strange. Gun owners would like to believe the assertions about Kellerman's statistics, because we believe they are seriously flawed, but disbelieve the assertions about Kleck's statistics. Yet asserting that Kleck's statistics justify owning or carrying a gun commits the same error that asserting that Kellerman's statistics justify not owning or banning guns. *Both treat the gun as an agent, with independent power to effect results.* In both cases, the gun has become a force, like a chemical, a drug or microbe, with independent power to cause results apart from our decisions, our character and purpose.

People, we are the agents. Guns are inanimate tools that serve our purposes.

Kellerman's statistics merely establish that guns are often used in, and are very useful and effective for, homicide. Kleck's statistics merely establish that guns are often used in, and are very useful and effective for, self-defense.

So it has been and ever will be. Only the numbers will change from year to year, state to state, country to country, culture to culture. It is we, however, who determine whether guns are used for good or ill in our lives, not the guns.

Both people who violently prey upon others and people who are serious about protecting themselves will own and use guns. In both cases, the guns are acquired and used because of their owners' decisions and values, intentions and will. In neither case do the guns "cause" violence or "result" in self-protection. Acquiring a gun will *enable* you to either commit violent crime or to defend yourself, but cannot *cause* these results. That depends on you.

The 20th Century social sciences have made great strides in teaching individuals to make decisions about their lives as policy decisions based on a statistical analysis of societal outcomes rather than on moral principles, to no discernible good effect. It is high time that people stopped thinking of themselves as governed by iron clad laws of human behavior presumed embodied in statistical facts, and began thinking of themselves as moral agents, with rights and duties, and the freedom to act. Instead of wondering what statistics reveal about the likelihood of what will or will not *happen* to us, it is time we began thinking about what we are going to *do*.

DEEP THINKING FROM TOP SOCIAL SCIENTISTS

Some of the nation's criminologists, roused by the increasing number of states reforming their laws to permit law-abiding citizens to carry concealed weapons, have begun to conduct research designed to "determine" whether these laws have any effect on crime. Or perhaps we should say, to create ammunition for opponents of concealed carry laws, who, to this point, have been sorely lacking statistics to "prove" just how misguided and dangerous these new concealed carry laws really are.

The first significant foray into this area was made in March, 1995 by the Violence Research Group at the University of Maryland, in a study funded by the Center for Disease Control and Prevention and titled "Easing Concealed Firearms Laws: Effect on Homicide in Three States." No doubt setting the tone for what follows, the very title of this report is inaccurate, for the study examines homicide rates in five *cities*, in three different states: Jacksonville, Tampa and Miami in Florida, Jackson, in Mississippi, and Portland, in Oregon.

The VRG's ground-breaking finding? The number of people killed by guns *rose* after laws making it easier for people to carry concealed weapons went into effect in four of these cities, despite the telling fact that the average number of homicides *by other means* remained steady. Specifically, the average number of homicides by gun increased by 74 percent in Jacksonville, 43 percent in Jackson, 22 percent in Tampa and 3 percent in Miami.

Although national rates for homicides also rose during the same period, the study pointed out that even when adjusted for the overall increase nationwide, the homicide rate increases in the test cities decreased only slightly. The implication the study wishes to create, then, is that the "relaxed" concealed carry laws, and not some factor generally at work in American society, was responsible for these increases.

The one city that did not neatly fit this explanation was Portland, where the researchers found that homicide rates fell about 12 percent after the concealed carry laws were relaxed. The researchers had, however, a ready alternative explanation.

Portland did not suffer the same fate as Jackson and the cities in Florida, they suggested, possibly because Oregon also enacted a law, at about the same time it relaxed its concealed carry law, to require background checks on firearms purchasers. "They tightened their gun-purchase laws about the same time as the concealed-weapons restrictions were relaxed, and that might have overwhelmed the effect of the relaxation," stated University of Maryland criminologist David McDowall.

In drawing a policy conclusion from his group's study, McDowall said "While advocates of these relaxed laws argue that they will prevent crime, and suggest that they have reduced homicides in areas that adopted them, we strongly suggest caution. When states weaken limits on concealed weapons, they may be giving up a simple and effective method of preventing firearm deaths." (*New York Times*, March 15, pg A23.)

Dr. Paul Blackmun, the NRA's criminologist, has drafted a short paper identifying the methodological flaws of the University of Maryland study. First, the researchers do not limit their examination of evidence to situations in which the carry of a weapon would be relevant. Thus, for example, the study does not report any data on homicides involving persons with carry permits — presumably because there were none. The authors simply hypothesize that, while the permit holders themselves may not be committing homicides, the fact that the law permits the law-abiding to carry might increase unlawful carrying by those inclined to criminal violence.

Furthermore, if you are trying to prove that a law permitting the carry of weapons increases homicides, you do not count homicides committed in the home, where the carrying of a weapon, and laws governing the carry of weapons, are irrelevant. The University of Maryland study, however, ignores the location of the homicides, and counts them all.

Second, the study fails to distinguish between unlawful homicides and justifiable or self-defense killings, again simply counting all deaths by firearms in its analysis. Thus, the study does not rule out that a portion of the increased deaths could be due to lawful self-defense, and not the criminal misuse of firearms.

Third, the methodology employed in the study does not isolate or test various other factors that could account for changes in homicide trends, such as demographic changes, sentencing or other legislative changes, or trends in drug trafficking. By failing to isolate, test for and rule out the extent to which these other trends affected the homicide rate, the authors fail to isolate the change in the concealed carry law as the likely cause of the increased homicide rate.

Fourth, the authors appear to have manipulated the time frames studied to reach a pre-ordained conclusion, picking different starting points for different cities and eliminating certain high homicide years which would have made the post-enactment years show a decline in homicide rates. And finally, the authors do not account for their selection of a few isolated cities or counties for analysis, while ignoring the results for the entire state.

State-wide, Florida's homicide rate fell 21 percent (through 1992) following enactment of the concealed carry law. The authors analysis does not explain why the homicide rates in the rest of

Florida fell so dramatically as to overwhelm the increased rates in a few localities, when all Floridians were living under the same law. How then, can the carry law be the cause of the increased rate?

When the cumulative effect of all these defects is considered, it is apparent that the University of Maryland study is not serious, disinterested social science, but partisan advocacy masquerading as science. The researchers, and the proponents of gun control who rely on their findings, know that most of the media and politicians are interested only in the conclusions, especially those that fit pre-existing beliefs, and will take the credentials of the researchers of as proof of the conclusions' validity.

They know, too, that the media, anti-gun politicians and even, perhaps, most people listening to the evening news or reading the newspaper will have little or no patience to hear about methodological flaws. It is enough, therefore, if the study provides opponents of concealed carry reform the appearance of a "rational" or "scientific" proof of the danger of these laws, and a reason to oppose concealed carry in the interest of public safety. In this sense, the University of Maryland study has succeeded, and has been cited in television shows debating the wisdom of concealed carry reform.

Far more interesting, to this author, are the underlying moral assumptions embodied in the VRG's policy conclusions. Consider what the authors of the VRG study are really saying. They mean for us to believe that a change in the law to permit law-abiding citizens who have been subjected to a background check to carry guns is the probable cause of more criminal homicides.

Since the permit holders are not themselves committing murder, how does this occur? There are at least two means, at least one of which is suggested by the VRG.

The fact that the law gives its blessing, as it were, to the carry of guns by the general populace creates a change in society's moral environment, so that carrying a gun is no longer taboo. Criminals, then, will be more likely to think there is nothing wrong in carrying a gun. Those who would not carry before will start, others will carry more often, and this will lead, inevitably to more criminal homicides.

Alternatively, or in addition, criminals, knowing that they are now more likely to encounter determined and life-threatening resistance from their victims, will be more likely to strike first, or react quickly, with lethal violence, in order to carry out their crimes with the least threat to themselves. Since anyone might be carrying concealed, they can no longer have the confidence they formerly possessed by selecting victims over whom they have an advantage in size, strength, youth or number.

Now, truth be told, it is possible, and not entirely implausible, that criminals might respond or react to concealed carry laws in one or both of these ways, although it may be difficult, if not impossible to "prove" through statistical analysis. Certainly criminals are going to react *somehow* to the fact that their victims may no longer be unarmed. It would be pure foolishness to think that, faced with the prospect of getting shot, they are simply all going to apply themselves at school, get jobs, settle down and raise a family.

Some may turn to burglary and theft, away from robbery, for example. Some may target tourists arriving from other lands, who assuredly will be unarmed. Some may plan their ambushes more carefully. Some may employ greater numbers. And some may become more violent, and strike first, and hard.

Let's assume then, for the sake of discussion, that the VRG is right, and that the passage of concealed carry laws destroys the taboo that formerly restrained at least some criminals from carrying and using guns, or causes criminals to resort to lethal violence more quickly. Faced now with these facts, what does the VRG recommend we all do? Retain the laws prohibiting concealed carry. Remain unarmed. Don't fight back. In short, better not make them mad, because then they might hurt us. We will all be better off, according to the VRG, if criminals can count on the fact that victims will be at their mercy, left only with the option of begging for their lives.

Greater safety, according to the VRG, lies in insuring that criminals can count on finding easy victims. The law should help satisfy criminals' need for easy victims by preventing the law-abiding from defending themselves with guns, so that criminals know that they can victimize us with as little violence as possible.

The VRG's policy recommendations thus permit the desire of criminals for easy victims to dictate the rights that the law will permit to the law-abiding. In the VRG's world, the needs of criminals dictate the conditions upon which the rest of us will be permitted to live.

Gun-control proponents who abhor the notion of an armed citizenry like to say that, "We shouldn't have to live that way." How, exactly, are the opponents of concealed carry laws at the VRG asking us to live?

WHOSE LIFE IS IT, ANYWAY?

Handgun Control, Inc. has a position paper available for distribution to members and grass-roots gun control lobbyists titled, "Carrying Concealed Weapons: Questions and Answers." The paper presents arguments against the adoption of the new "shall issue" licensing laws.

In general, the new CCW laws provide that an applicant who is not a convicted felon, mentally ill or a chronic or habitual user of alcohol or controlled substances, who passes a fingerprint and background check and meets certain other objective criteria *must* be given a permit to carry.

In the past ten years, approximately 24 states have adopted such laws, replacing discretionary licensing systems in which issuance of permit depended on satisfying the licensing authority that the applicant had a special "need" or "reason" to carry and was of "good moral character."

The HCI paper begins by reporting that, according to the NRA, the justification for the new CCW laws is that they will decrease violent crime. The HCI paper then proceeds to provide arguments why it is unrealistic to expect that (i) more people carrying guns will reduce crime, and (ii) ordinary citizens will be able to defend themselves.

The paper cites a study explaining that criminologist Gary Kleck's claim that guns are used approximately 1.5 to 2.5 million times a year in defense of life or property is wrong, and claims, based on a University of Maryland study, that the real number is about 65,000.

Next, the paper reports the finding of a New England Journal of Medicine study that a gun in the home is 43 times more likely to cause the death of a family member or a friend than a criminal. In other word, guns are hardly ever used successfully in self-defense, and they are more dangerous to their owners than to criminals.

As further evidence that laws permitting concealed carry will not reduce crime, we are told that the police oppose them:

". . . law enforcement across the country has consistently opposed these efforts. Obviously, if law enforcement believed that CCW laws would lessen crime, they would support them. Instead, under these laws, police officers must assume that everyone is carrying a firearm and willing to take the law into their own hands; every verbal confrontation, at a bar, in a restaurant, at a traffic stop, could become a potential gun battle."

HCI then presents evidence that, it believes, establishes that it is unrealistic to expect that licensees will be able to defend themselves: not all states with CCW laws require applicants to have taken firearms training. Of those that do, most (HCI reports correctly) do not even require that the applicant have fired his weapon as part of the training. This shortcoming is all the more serious, HCI implies, given that even highly trained police are sometimes unable to defend themselves:

"Even the most highly trained law enforcement professionals are not always able to protect themselves with firearms - a fact that was tragically emphasized with the November, 1994 shooting inside the District of Columbia

Police Headquarters. Three law enforcement officers, including two FBI agents, were killed by a gunman who opened fire on them. The thought that average citizens will somehow be better able to successfully defend themselves more effectively than our nations' trained professionals is absurd."

The implication appears to be that CCW licensees who try to defend themselves with firearms are going to be killed far more often than law enforcement officers because of insufficient training. This may or may not be true, but it bears asking why "average citizens," as HCI likes to call us, should have to demonstrate that we will be better able or at least as able to defend themselves successfully as the nation's police before obtaining a carry license.

Suppose we grant that CCW licensees won't be as successful in defending themselves with firearms as are the police — that is, that more, on a percentage basis, will be killed trying to defend themselves than occurs with the police.

Isn't it the licensee's life to defend? It is not HCI's nor the governments' place to tell him that he will be better off if he doesn't even try, or bother. Where does the moral authority come from for one individual, or group, to tell another person how to make this decision?

We could make various rebuttals to each of HCI's claims, but let's try, instead, to discern the general strategies employed in these arguments. There are at least two. First, HCI repeatedly points out the numerous dangers and possible horrible results that might occur if CCW laws are passed and mere "average citizens" begin carrying arms, in order to prove that these laws are a bad idea.

The police will have to assume the worst about us, arguments could become gun battles, permit holders might have their guns taken away from them and used against them, licensees might be killed more frequently than the police trying to defend themselves because of insufficient training, and other assorted calamities.

This strategy depends, for its success, on frightening or over-whelming the targeted audience with the list of horribles, and hopes the audience mistakes what has been presented as *possible* for the results that will most likely occur.

But we don't have to rely on speculation about what *might* happen if these laws are passed. We have at least 10 years of evidence, studiously avoided by HCI, about what *has* happened in states that have passed these laws. Fender benders and everyday arguments do *not* erupt into gun battles involving permit holders. Permit holders do *not* resort to settling arguments with hot lead.

Notwithstanding HCI's worry that permit holders will not be able to defend themselves as well as the police, Department of Justice statistics — uncontested by gun control advocates — indicate that people who defend themselves with firearms are less likely to suffer injury than those who don't resist or resist with other means. Persons who defend themselves with guns have them taken away from them by the assailant *less than one percent* of the time.

Yes, it is true, the horrible consequences HCI predicts might occur. Anything is possible. But the historical evidence reveals that they are likely to be *extremely* rare, and decidedly *not* the norm.

The second strategy is more subtle and, if not caught, more damaging. HCI says that the NRA claims that carry laws should be passed because they will reduce crime. (The paper cites no source for this claim; we do not know if the NRA in fact makes this claim.) HCI then sets out to prove why it is unrealistic to believe this will occur.

The argument implied in HCI's presentation is that ordinary citizens ought not to be licensed to carry arms unless in fact permitting them to carry would lead to a decrease in crime. In other words, the individual ought not to be permitted the privilege of carrying arms to defend himself unless there is first proof that society as a whole will benefit (the violent crime rate will go down).

You, dear reader, do not *deserve* to carry to defend your life unless it can first be demonstrated that, taking the actions of all licensees together, the violent crime rate will go down. In other words, your right to life depends on the statistical outcome of what others, including criminals, do.

HCI has couched the debate in terms of a utilitarian argument about the greatest good for the greatest number, and shifted it away from a debate about each individual's right to life. Arguing with HCI whether CCW laws will or won't reduce crime accepts HCI's terms of the debate. If HCI can sufficiently muddy the waters so that it is not provable whether CCW laws in fact decrease crime, then, on these terms, there is no reason to pass such laws, for there is no provable benefit to society.

Rather than making your right to life depend on prior reasonably good proof that the collective outcome of the actions of the majority will produce a favorable statistical result, consider an alternative moral ground for action.

Consider that the right to defend your life does not depend on, and has nothing to do with, how high or low the violent crime rate is. Consider that your right has nothing whatsoever to do with whether carrying guns does or does not reduce the violent crime rate or how many people do or do not defend themselves with guns or how well or poorly they have done so.

Why should the majority tell you that your life must be forfeit if the crime rates are so low as to not be worth thinking about? Why should that majority be able to tell you that your life must be forfeit if your carrying of arms won't produce any measurable benefit *for them*? Why should the majority tell you that your life must be forfeit if you might not perform as well as the police? Whose life is it, anyway?

UTILITY, DESTROYER OF RIGHTS

John Lott, a professor at the University of Chicago School of Law, has done us the great service of undertaking the most rigorous and comprehensive study of the relationship between violent crime and "shall-issue" concealed carry laws ever made. Indeed, it is the most comprehensive American criminological analysis *ever* undertaken, both in terms of the amount of data it analyzes and summarizes, and the number of factors it isolates to test for causal relationships. His findings are summed up in the title of the book: *More Guns, Less Crime.* It is a milestone in the history of the gun control debate, is good reading notwithstanding the occasional technical discussion, and contains revelations that destroy a fair portion of modern gun control mythology.

After a few introductory remarks about criminological research on guns and crime, Lott's book launches on a more expansive, and accessible, explanation of the Lott-Mustard study, published in 1997. The results of that study were widely reported in the general press. Analyzing extensive data from all 3,054 counties in the United States throughout the period 1977 -1992, Lott and Mustard found that when shall-issue licensing laws went into effect in a county, murders fell, on average, by 7.65 percent, rapes fell by 5.2

percent robberies fell by 2.2 percent, and aggravated assaults fell by 7 percent. If all counties in the United States had had shall issue licensing laws in effect, then, in 1992 there would have been1,414 fewer murders, 4,177 fewer rapes, 11,898 fewer robberies, and 60,363 fewer aggravated assaults.

On the other hand, property crime rates increased 2.7 percent after the passage of shall-issue concealed carry laws, indicating that there would have been an additional 247,165 property crimes in 1992. Lott concludes that criminals appear to respond to the threat of being shot by victims carrying concealed weapons by engaging instead in less risky, nonconfrontational property crimes.

Lott updates the original study by incorporating the evidence from 1992 - 1994; his original findings hold. Here, then is hard statistical evidence that the new concealed carry laws save lives and prevent physical and psychical harm, and confer a benefit on society at large.

The Lott-Mustard study made a notable advance in criminological research methodology by focusing on county level data as the unit for comparison, rather than on states. This was done because states are too large and heterogeneous, and thus prone to generate false associations. Lott notes this is particularly true with respect to concealed carry laws. It is well known that states which have discretionary licensing systems do not apply those laws consistently. Permits are more freely given to citizens in rural counties, and are difficult to impossible to obtain in suburban and urban counties. Thus, passage of a "shall issue" licensing law effects little or no real change in the practices of issuing permits in rural counties, but radically alters practices in cities and in counties with large populations. Looking at the data only at the state level, then, would be like mixing apples and oranges, and obscure the real results.

Significantly, Lott's study found that, while all counties generally benefited from the passage of shall issue licensing laws, they had the greatest deterrent effect in counties with a population in excess of 100,000 and attendant high crime rates. High crime areas thus stand to benefit most from laws permitting citizens to carry handguns for self-defense.

It is important to note that these results were obtained after factoring out and measuring (by a process known as regression analysis) the effects of other factors that could have accounted for reductions in the violent crime rate, such as changes in population, changes in arrest and conviction rates, changes in income levels, racial and age breakdowns, and changes resulting from passage of other gun control laws. Thus, Lott's conclusions about the deterrent effect of shall issue licensing laws are reached *after* measuring (and factoring out) the extent to which reductions in the violent crime rate during the 1977- 1992 period were attributable to these *other* factors, such as migration of population out of a county.

No gun control study has ever gone this far in identifying and analyzing the effect of so many factors that can account for changes in the crime rate. This has twofold significance. First, Lott is capable of assigning measured significance to each factor's contribution to the total reduction in the violent crime rate. For example, he was able to determine that the passage of waiting period and background check laws like Brady during this period had *no* deterrent effect on violent crime, and that the single most important factor in deterring violent crime is the *arrest* rate. Findings such as these have obvious policy implications for the direction of criminal justice system resources.

Second, by isolating the effects of other factors, he establishes that it is far more likely that there is in fact a causal relationship (and not merely a correlation) between passage of concealed carry laws and a reduction in the violent crime rate. Thus, Lott has raised the bar very high indeed for critics who want to prove that Lott's results are really only a false or apparent correlation and that the reduction in crime he attributes to concealed carry laws is really due to some other factor. They must find that factor, and to date they have not been able to do so.

Lott has made his entire data set available to all comers, and his findings have been independently replicated by numerous criminologists. Several criminologists have, however, assailed his work on technical and other grounds, and one chapter of Lott's book is devoted to answering those who have questioned the validity of his findings. Without going into detail here, many of the critics' arguments are highly revealing of the manner in which anti-gun researchers endeavor to brush off pro-gun findings: they raise a question or suggest a possible theory that would, if true, undermine the study's findings. Then, without endeavoring to do the hard work of determining whether their theory has any support in the evidence, simply leave the question or theory hanging there to suggest that, because the question can be asked or the theory proposed, the findings are flawed. The criticisms of Jens Ludwig, a criminologist at Georgetown, generally fall into this class. Lott's answers demolish his critics' positions.

The most entertaining chapter in the book, well worth the price of the book for its instructive value alone, is Lott's documented account of anti-gun organizations' reactions to the publication of the original Lott-Mustard study. There, Lott recounts the instances in which his critics were issuing reports to the press that his work was seriously flawed before they had even read it! This part of the story also discloses the cozy relationship between members of the press and anti-gun researchers. Lott was shocked to hear one brag to him that he could pick up a phone and in minutes have his viewpoint printed in newspapers the following day. Ah, the scientific method in action! Ah, the glories of an open mind!

While Lott's book is a milestone in the criminological study of gun control, it would be a shame if its effect and use were limited to establishing a very strong factual case that concealed carry laws save lives, for the book provides strong material for raising another, equally interesting examination. It begins where Lott's book ends: "While people have strong views on either side of this debate, . . .[i]n the final analysis, one concern unites us all: Will allowing law-abiding citizens to carry concealed handguns save lives? The answer is yes."

Here, Lott credits all parties in the debate as, fundamentally, sharing a common value: the desire to preserve the greatest number of lives. The gun control debate is thus reduced to well-meaning people arguing over the best or most prudent means to accomplish that good and common goal, the answer to which, in turn, can be provided by a comprehensive analysis that discloses truly whether means A (gun control) or means B (the liberty to defend oneself) saves the most lives. In fact, however, Lott's own experience with the intellectual dishonesty of his opponents, as reported in his book, ought to have caused him to question this assumption.

Handgun Control, Inc. and the Center to Prevent Gun Violence have not abandoned their opposition to the passage of shall-issue concealed carry laws, despite Lott's findings and despite the absence (thus far) of a viable basis for denying the validity of those findings. Given the strength of Lott's analysis and evidence, and gun control activists' initial, prejudicial dismissal and insupportable criticism of his work, we have good reason to question whether gun control advocates are, really or fundamentally, driven by a concern with saving the most lives.

Champion of the greatest good

Let us imagine a man whose great guiding star in questions of governance is, what policy produces the greatest good for the greatest number? What policy, enacted into law, will save the most lives, and avert the most harm? We will suppose him absolutely honest and resolute in his commitment to this overarching value, by which mark all others are judged and prioritized.

This man, let us suppose, has read the results of gun control studies; he knows that guns are 43 times more likely to cause the death of an acquaintance or family member than an intruder in his home, and so forth. For years he has been a staunch and vigorous advocate of greater gun control, convinced that it will save lives, and reduce suffering.

Now comes the day when he reads of a new study in his newspaper, by John Lott, who has carried out what is apparently the most thorough, exhaustive and rigorous criminological study of guns and crime in the history of mankind. Amazingly, the findings indicate that permitting people to carry guns to defend themselves saves more lives! Deeply disturbed, our hero visits his library at the first opportunity to read this report. He must know, you see, must truly know, as best a man can know, what the truth is, for the consequence of being wrong is that he mistakenly advocates policies that actually result in greater harm, that actually result in people's deaths!

The critical point is that our champion of the greatest good assumes the right, or at least the power, to decide for others how they may and may not act (although his avowed principle declares that he does so only for the greater good). Having assumed, and exercised, that power, he bears the responsibility (morally, not legally) of deciding wrongly for others. Thus, if he supports and advocates laws which coerce others into living in the manner he believes likely to secure the best aggregate outcome (such as by prohibiting them from carrying arms to defend themselves), he bears the moral responsibility for a wrong decision. He himself becomes a source of harm in the world; if the decision concerns a matter of life or death, he has blood on his hands!

Perhaps he is not so subtle as to fully understand this; yet we have posited that he is sincerely devoted to his principle of acting (and compelling others to act) in order to maximize saved lives and minimize harm to the innocent, and this is sufficient. He knows he must get it right, to the extent that is humanly possible, if he is to actually achieve his highest, most worthy goal.

So it is that he is greatly disturbed by Lott's work, for being wrong must place him in an agony of spirit, and being right must be his sincerest wish, as it is essential to judge rightly how to save the most others and how best to alleviate suffering. At the first opportunity, then, he rushes to the library to read the new work. He is not a criminologist, he cannot make an independent test of the data for himself, yet he must admit the case is very strong.

He reads the critics of the study and he reads Lott's response to the critics. He notices that not even Lott's critics are prepared to argue, in the face of Lott's evidence and analysis, that shall issue carry laws result in greater crime or more harm; the most they will argue is that Lott is wrong in asserting that they reduce crime. Thus, in case of a doubt, it seems the matter should be resolved in favor of Lott, for no one argues that there is a demonstrable downside to shall issue concealed carry laws, but there is a significant potential upside.

Perhaps he is fully convinced by Lott's findings. The fact that he was wrong is painful to him, and tears at his conscience. For you see, he now knows that when he labored against concealed carry laws, he worked against the greatest good, he worked for policies that resulted in greater harm, more deaths!

But now that he does know, he also knows his duty! Yes, he must *recommend* and support such laws. Perhaps he must go further and seek laws that actually *compel* people to carry concealed, just as he once sought laws to *prohibit* them from doing so, for he desires to force people to act so as to produce the greatest good for the greatest number. To make up for his previous error, and his failure to realize the highest good, he throws himself into his new project with renewed and greater fervor.

Perhaps after reading Lott's critics and Lott's response, he is not entirely sure that Lott's findings are correct, yet he also now knows there is no solid evidence that these laws produce harm, and that there is quite a good chance that people who say these laws are beneficial are correct. He therefore has no basis for asserting, as objective truth, that laws that prohibit the carry of concealed arms are for the aggregate greater good. In fact, the opposite appears more probable. At a minimum, then, he must speak out against anyone who asserts that laws prohibiting the carry of arms are for the greater good, as having insufficient basis for such claim.

In the mean time, having no knowledge of which means (prohibition or liberty) will in truth produce the greater good, he lacks an objective basis for insisting upon how others should act. Oh miserable man! He will have to bear to let others decide for themselves while he waits for the social scientists to sort things out! Yes, he will have to stop telling others what to do. He will have to shut up.

Surely, were men sincerely devoted to the principle of the greatest good for the greatest number, their behavior would roughly approximate that of our champion of the greatest good. Yet how comical! Nowhere do we see this happening. The gun control organizations are not troubled enough by the possibility that they may be wrong even to read Lott's report before issuing denunciations.

HCI shows no crisis of confidence; it continues as before, working against shall issue licensing laws, pretending Lott doesn't exist! Could it be that gun control proponents are not the humanitarians they think themselves, that they affect a greater solicitude for their fellow man than they actually have? Could it be that they are not really interested in the greatest good for the greatest number, but seek to control guns for other reasons?[1]

I by no means wish to imply that supporters of an individual right to bear arms lay greater claim to humanitarian impulses, or are more truly champions of the greatest good. I do mean, however, that the fact that Lott's work has wrought no change of heart in gun control proponents offers a fair demonstration of the truth of the following proposition: The desire to save the most lives is not the driving force or principal goal of the overwhelming majority of gun control activists, whatever assertions they may make to the contrary.

Given that a large, perhaps overwhelming majority of gun control advocates continue to staunchly oppose shall issue concealed carry laws in the face of rigorous, strong evidence that such laws save lives and avert harm, it can be fairly maintained that saving lives is *not* the foremost or deciding factor in their desire to impose gun control. In fact, it can be fairly maintained that they want gun

---

1 It is possible for gun control proponents to counter this argument by saying that while concealed weapon laws may save lives here and there, guns taken as a whole in all aspects of life result, on net balance, in greater loss of life; that, therefore, while concealed weapon laws taken in isolation may be favorable, guns as a whole must be opposed to achieve a true aggregate good. However, such a claim merely directs the analysis to a discussion of Gary Kleck's work, which shows that guns are used defensively about 2 to 2.5 million times a year, far more often in defense of life and property than in the taking of life and property. Kleck's work, too, must of necessity produce a similar crisis of confidence for any gun control advocate who is a true champion of the aggregate greatest good.

control *despite* strong evidence that gun control costs (net) lives.

If this analysis is correct, though, why do gun control advocates invest so much energy in studies to prove that guns cause more harm than good, and in trumpeting the results? Why do they try so hard to convince others to accept the findings as a guide to action and legislation, when they themselves will not accept them if the findings turn out to be at variance with *their* sentiments? Why do they expect others to act on the basis of an ethical principle which they will not take as their own guide?

The utilitarian destruction of rights

There are several reasons, but the most important is this: "proving" that gun use creates more harm than good provides the moral and political justification for coercing gun owners into acting on the basis of gun control proponents' views of right and wrong. Without a colorable, fact-based claim that gun control is for our own, greater good, imposing gun control, through law, is simply and too obviously the raw exercise of power by one group in society forcing its mere opinions, sentiments or faith on another.

For example, it was necessary to "find" (more accurately, to invent) "scientific" evidence that second hand smoke was a serious health hazard to non-smokers before launching the war on smoking. Once this "evidence" was produced, non-smokers could claim that they were acting in everyone's best interests by curbing smoking. Smokers are effectively silenced because, by defending their desire to smoke, they are regarded as arguing for a right to harm others. Smokers then lose their "rights" (or their "rights" are subordinated to the rights of nonsmokers) because there is no right to harm others. Because smokers have thus been shown to be engaged in conduct harmful to others and not merely to themselves, they are transformed into anti-social misfits.

The utilitarian justification for prohibiting smoking (the greater good, health, for the greater number, nonsmokers) is thus far more defensible than would be a claim of right to control smokers' behavior simply on the basis of the aesthetic sensibilities of nonsmokers, now in the majority and able to reflect their desires in law, who feel that smoking is a disgusting, dirty, low-class habit. Nonsmokers may in fact be motivated by just such sentiments, but the epidemiological evidence that smoking is harmful to non-smokers provides a "scientific" and altruistic basis for imposing their will on smokers.

Similarly, gun control proponents seek to establish a "scientific" finding that guns work greater harm than good in order to obtain a moral and political justification for coercing gun owners into complying with a strict regime of gun control or for outright prohibition. It little matters that they do not care if it is true, that they are in fact driven by sentiments unrelated to whether or not more people are lost to gun violence than are saved by gun use. They need a utilitarian justification to impose their will on others.

In short, gun control advocates need utilitarianism because *utilitarianism trumps individual rights*. For the modern democratic state, utilitarianism is *the* ethical doctrine that serves to both justify governmental action and supersede individual rights.

The gun control debate is a clash between these two discrete and utterly incompatible ethics. While even gun rights advocates seek to establish that the right to keep and bear arms will bring about the greatest good for the greatest number, utilitarianism is neither consistent nor compatible with a philosophy that individuals have certain fundamental rights. It is, in fact, completely destructive of a philosophy of individual right.

It should be obvious, but apparently is not, that the utilitarian ethic subordinates the individual's liberty to a desired aggregate result. "The greatest good for the greatest number" is, by definition, a formula for subordinating the desires or conduct of the one to the greater good of the many. Utilitarianism would be consistent with an individual right ethic only in the extreme and utterly improbable case where there are no two people anywhere who have a greater good than the individual. Since the utilitarian ethic is, also, by definition, majoritarian (the desires of the greatest number among the competing pluralities ruling the day), the majority (or the largest of the pluralities) decides whether or not its own perceived good is greater than, and thus supersedes, any particular individual's notion of his own good.[2] In both process and result, therefore, the utilitarian ethic is inherently inconsistent with an ethic of individual right — that is, an ethic that claims that there are certain matters which individuals may decide and act upon on their own, independent of the "will of the majority," and regardless of whether a majority perceive their own benefit to lie elsewhere.

Now, if individuals are permitted to have certain "rights" only so long as their exercise of those rights is perceived to serve or bring about the greatest good of the greatest number, they in fact have no "inalienable" or "individual" rights. In this circumstance, the utilitarian ethic in fact has become is the final arbiter of whether or not an individual keeps his liberty. As soon as a majority (or the largest plurality) perceives its benefit to lie elsewhere, the individual's liberty or "right" will be taken away, subordinated to the greater good of the greater number. The individual, then, has no rights independent of the desires of the many and their perceptions of what best serves their overall interests. The individual keeps his "rights" only so long as the greatest number among competing pluralities perceives that that right serves their own self interest.

So it is that when we defend the right to own and carry firearms with utilitarian arguments like those of John Lott, we are in no sense defending an individual right. We are, instead, simply trying to convince a majority of our fellow citizens to permit us to exercise such freedom because there's something in it for them. This is an attempt to purchase liberty, and an implicit admission that our "rights" are subordinate to, and dependent upon, the desires and wishes of our fellow citizens.

---

2 Some would argue that, in theory, utilitarianism does not have to be majoritarian, that there is no reason, for example, that a single, all-wise philosopher king could not independently decide what the greatest good for the greatest number is, and impose laws designed to achieve it on his unwitting, unwilling subjects, even though they themselves do not perceive that it is for their own good. For reasons we need not go into here, that argument is unsound. However, regardless of its truth, that is not how the doctrine works in the modern, democratic state.

Enlightened human sacrifice

Let's recapitulate. Thus far, we have argued that there are two discrete ethical doctrines at war in the gun control debate: social utilitarianism ("the greatest good for the greatest number") and individual rights. Our thesis is that these two philosophies are incompatible and, further, that in a kind of Gresham's Law of the moral universe, utilitarianism drives out deontology.[3] If this be correct, it follows that it is impossible to secure or validate individual rights on utilitarian grounds. In fact, any attempt to do so completely negates not only the existence of the individual right, but also the very concept of individual right. This point is so fundamental to understanding, not only the nature of the gun control debate, but also the ethical currency with which modern democratic governments purchase the liberty of their citizens (who, more properly speaking, thereby become subjects) that we must examine more closely how utilitarianism destroys individual rights.

Under an individual right ethic, individuals may not be treated solely as a means to an end but must also be treated, in Kant's words, as "ends in themselves." The individual has an inherent dignity because he possesses a free will, that is, the capacity of autonomously exercising ethical freedom. Since each man must be recognized as having such dignity, the fact that one man abuses his freedom, and acts unethically to the detriment of his fellow man, provides no justification for curbing the ethical autonomy of another.

In legal rather than moral terms, the fact that some men abuse their freedom provides no justification for imposing a prior restraint upon the exercise of another's liberty. (He may, though, be punished, *after the fact*, if he has acted with intent to harm his fellow man.)

For the sake of discussion, let's assume that keeping and bearing arms suitable for self-defense is a bona fide individual right. If

---

3 This is because utilitarianism is founded in desire, and so easily overwhelms, while the deontological requires subordination of desire to the moral law, and so requires what is far more difficult — faith.

122

so, the fact that 100,000 people a year murder others with firearms, while one man alone uses a firearm to save a life, provides no basis for curbing the individual liberty to own and bear arms. *Each* individual *must*, because of his inherent, autonomous ethical freedom, be respected as an end in himself; no prior restraint may be imposed upon his right to keep and bear firearms.

Actually we can go further. Under an individual right view, the fact that 100,000 people a year murder innocents with firearms, and *no one* uses a firearm to protect himself or others provides no basis for a prior restraint. Individuals must still be possessed of a right to own firearms because their ethical freedom contains the *potentiality* of using firearms for good. That is, people can use this tool for good, if they turn to it with a good will. The key points are these: the individual may not be used solely as a means to achieving the ends of others; and the individual's right does not depend on *others* having, in the aggregate, used such right to the good, providing a net benefit to society as a whole.

Now utilitarianism will have none of this. Utilitarianism is a results-driven ethic, that is, it is driven by the desire to secure a specified result, a particular "greatest good" desired by the greatest number. Utilitarianism thus concerns itself with gaming the *outcome* of the exercise of man's freedom. By definition, all matters, all concerns are necessarily *subordinate* to the acquisition of the "greatest good." It is not content to leave men alone in their freedom, to let the chips fall where they may, with some using their freedom wisely and others to the harm of their fellow man, and addressing the harm done after the fact.

It seeks to control or circumscribe the exercise of man's freedom in order to achieve a particular desired aggregate result: it wants those 100,000 murders to disappear, or at least, to have more lives saved than lost. Thus, it is willing to, and does, use individuals solely as a means to an end.

Because it concerns itself with securing a desired aggregate outcome, whether the individual is permitted liberty to act depends on whether his fellow citizens are, in the aggregate, using their liberty to achieve the desired good. If not, the individual's liberty may be curbed, or re-directed. The individual's freedom depends on how *others* behave, and is defined and circumscribed with reference to the results that *others* achieve. This, of course, is the polar opposite of what people generally understand having an "individual right" to mean.

Take, for example, gun prohibition as a means of eliminating gun crime, on the assumption that the evidence is clear that if gun crime can be eliminated more people's lives will be saved than lost (the avowed greatest good assumed to be the preservation of the greatest number of lives). All are deprived of arms to eliminate the harm caused by those who would otherwise abuse their freedom by using firearms to commit crimes. Let's assume this law works, that is, in fact achieves its goal of eliminating all gun crime, and thereby maximizes lives saved.

It is evident from this example, first, that the individual's liberty to own firearms depends on whether sufficient others are using them to produce desirable results. In this case, we have posited that they are not, that is, that more people are dying from gun crimes than are being saved by persons defending themselves with guns. The utilitarian "solution" to maximize aggregate welfare is thus to deprive all individuals of the liberty to own firearms. The scope of an individual's freedom, then, is not a function of the respect due him as independent agent having free will, and does not depend on his own conduct, but is instead a function of how his fellow citizens behave and the results they achieve.

Second, the individual's private good is not merely subordinate to realization of the aggregate greatest good, but is freely sacrificed to securing that greatest good. The obverse of the fact that more lives are saved by gun prohibition is that some, having been deprived of an effective tool of self-defense, will of necessity *lose* their lives, so that others, admittedly more numerous, will live. In short, some are sacrificed freely so that others, comprising a greater number, may live.

Utilitarianism sanctions human sacrifice, both great and small, as long as it is for "the greatest good of the greatest number." That is, utilitarianism justifies using some merely as a means to the fulfillment of others' ends, so long as those who are to be sacrificed are not too numerous. The individual thus has no right to life; that life has become so much raw material to be disposed of in pursuit of the *aggregate* greatest good.[4]

In contrast, a philosophy of individual right is not results-driven and therefore does not sanction human sacrifice in favor of the highest good desired by the greatest number. An approach that rests on man's freedom cannot, by definition, be driven by outcome or result: if men are left free, *the outcome will be left variable!* Of necessity, an approach that rests in freedom cannot possibly guaranty a specified, favorable outcome, either individually or in the aggregate. It cannot, therefore, promise safety, security, a reduction in violent crime, etc. Such concerns are blissfully beside the point, for the point is precisely to respect each individual as an "end in himself."

The approach here is not to argue the superiority of individual rights over utilitarianism, or vice versa, or to defend one against the other. Here we have examined the differences between the two competing ethical systems solely in order to make it plain that they are heterogeneous and incompatible.

The implication of this, though, may be difficult for gun and other rights advocates to bear: *utilitarian arguments cannot possibly justify a claim of individual right.* Any attempt to justify the maintenance or existence of an individual right on the basis of utilitarian arguments, i.e., on the basis that giving scope to such freedom provides a net benefit to society at large, in fact contradicts the claim that individuals have any fundamental right.

If individual rights must be justified or defended by proof of delivery of an aggregate social benefit (e.g., fewer murders, a decrease in the violent crime rate, safer streets, etc.), they are not

---

4 It should be obvious that if an individual's very right to life cannot survive within social utilitarianism, no lesser right will survive either. Within utilitarianism, individuals have *no* rights.

"individual rights" in the classic sense, for such rights were thought to be "inalienable," inhering in the subject solely because of his autonomous will. "Rights" that rest on utilitarian foundations are, at best, provisional liberties subject to continual redefinition and outright revocation upon the basis of ongoing analysis of the behavior of one's fellow citizens and the results they are achieving.

While gun owners may trumpet studies, like those by John Lott or Gary Kleck, showing the net good associated with gun ownership, those who seek to justify the right to keep and bear arms on the basis that the right best serves society by saving more lives and averting more harm than its opposite (gun control) in fact contradict the notion that individuals have a fundamental right to own and carry arms. These "numbers" arguments move within an ethic that (i) tacitly accepts that the desires of the majority to acquire their highest good determines the amount of liberty permitted to an individual, and (ii) defines the scope of an individual's liberty by reference to the behavior of others, and not on the basis of the individual's own conduct or ethical capacity. By arguing in this manner, they are conceding that their very lives are at the disposal of, and bound in service to, the desires of the majority.

The Second Amendment

"L'homme vivant sous la servitude des lois prend sans s'en douter une âme d'escave." The man who lives under the servitude of laws takes, without suspecting it, the soul of a slave.

George Ripert
Le Déclin du Droit.
Etude sur la législation contemporaine

THE SECOND AMENDMENT IS DEAD

In the '60s, a group of clergy gained considerable notoriety by boldly announcing that God is dead. Looking back, what is interesting about this event was the manner in which the clergymen's statement was misunderstood. Indignant believers rushed to God's defense, loudly proclaiming that He did, indeed, exist, and that they believed in Him.

Yet the clergymen were not claiming that God did not exist; they believed He did. The were making a far more disturbing, and damning claim: that even those who professed to believe in God lived their lives as though He were dead. God's existence, and their avowed belief in Him, made no apparent difference in the way in which they lived their lives. Those who believed in God acted, for all intents and purposes, no differently than those who disavowed His existence.

These recollections came to mind as I thought about the recent Supreme Court decision in *United States v. Lopez,* and the appellate argument recently made by pro-gun advocates in two cases challenging the constitutionality of the Brady Act, *Koog v. United States* and *McGee v. United States.*

In *Lopez*, the Supreme Court struck down the Gun Free School Zone Act of 1990, the law making it a federal crime to possess a firearm on school property. Recognizing that the federal government had no general police power which would authorize such a law, the Court rejected the federal government's claim that the gun ban was a proper exercise of Congress' power "to regulated Commerce . . . among the States." (Article I, Section 8, Clause 3, U.S. Constitution.)

In a recent argument before the U.S. Fifth Circuit Court of Appeals in *Koog* and *McGee*, noted Second Amendment scholar and author Stephen Halbrook maintained that the federal government had no authority to require local law enforcement to conduct background checks on prospective firearm purchasers. The exercise of such a general police power was reserved, under the 10th Amendment to the Constitution, to the states.

Similarly, recent court challenges to state and local assault weapon bans were brought on grounds that the bans violated due process (due to vagueness of the definition of an "assault weapon") or denied equal protection of the laws by arbitrarily banning some semiautomatic weapons but not others that are functionally indistinguishable).

Lopez, Koog and *McGee* continue the modern trend of challenging gun control laws on any and all constitutional grounds — except the Second Amendment. Fearing that the courts will hold that the Second Amendment does not protect an individual right to keep and bear arms, pro-gun advocates refrain from asserting claims under the Second Amendment. This strategy evidently seeks to "preserve" the Second Amendment by avoiding the creation of unfavorable precedents, until the political climate or the ideology of judges on the bench changes, and a strong, sweeping affirmation of the Second Amendment is assured.

Yet the notion that silence somehow "preserves" the Second Amendment is ludicrous. Failing time and again to assert a fundamental right in circumstances where it is meant, and ought, to apply surely creates as much a precedent as asserting it only to suffer defeat. In legal terms, such silence creates a "negative pregnant," that is, creates a clear implication that the Second Amendment does not apply. After all, the normal course of conduct for a party in a court contest is to set forth all possible grounds of defense or assault, especially those which dispose decisively of the issue at hand.

If expediency and political calculations determine when one can or will assert a right which is supposedly fundamental, than that right is no longer fundamental. If no federal court in the land will enforce the Second Amendment, and if even those who profess to be its strongest believers will not assert it in their defense in a court of law, then the Second Amendment is dead.

It is dead because it ceased long ago to live in the hearts of Americans. Yes, some 70 million Americans own firearms, and tens of millions use firearms recreationally. Although many profess belief in the right guaranteed by the Second Amendment, most act, for all intents and purposes, no differently than those who disavow the right.

Consider the evidence of the numbers. Despite the fact that concerted efforts have been made for some time now to curb the right to own and use firearms, only 3.4 million — less than 5 percent of all gun owners and less than 3 percent of all adult Americans — are members of the principal organization dedicated to preserving the right to own or use firearms. Indeed, the mere fact that the NRA's strategy and source of success is terrorizing politicians with the specter of defeat indicates, in and of itself, that the Second Amendment is dead in Congress and the state legislatures.

Nor is the fact that more and more states are passing favorable concealed carry laws as hopeful a sign as it appears. In Florida, where the law has been in effect for eight years, there are only approximately 200,000 permits outstanding — less than 3 percent of Florida's adult population. Hardly a rousing number putting their rights into practice.

More telling than the numbers, however, is the fact that the new carry laws provide for concealed carry. Yes, there are tactical reasons why carrying concealed is safer than open carry. But there are also tactical reasons for carrying openly, and it is considerably more comfortable! Regardless, the tactical considerations governing handgun deployment are not the driving force for concealed carry reform.

In Virginia, where a new concealed carry law just went into effect, it was, and still is, perfectly legal to carry openly. Yet no one, other than the police and security guards, does so. Why will Virginians only carry concealed? Because they, and all others who have pushed for concealed carry, know perfectly well that the sight of an ordinary citizen going about his daily business with a firearm at his side will strike fear into the hearts of the overwhelming majority of fellow citizens. They know — we all know — that openly carrying a firearm will be regarded as unseemly, if not outright insane, and will draw scorn, derision and the attention of the police.

The push for concealed carry thus essentially rests on the desire of gun owners who wish to protect themselves outside their homes — to hide their shame. The reformers' answer to the great majority of citizens' fear of an unauthorized someone with a gun is the rather flippant, disdainful, "What you don't know won't hurt you." Hardly noble or honorable conduct.

In short, even the success stories, whether it be court victories like *Lopez* or concealed carry reform, prove the case: the Second Amendment is dead. "True believers" are a very, very small minority.

Because they are intensely motivated, well organized, well funded and play electoral politics well, they have achieved victories all out of proportion to their numbers. But interest group politics, and legislative and court victories will not inspire unbelievers, nor revive the right, which lives, if at all, in the human breast. Perhaps we should stop parading around the corpse of the Second Amendment — the dead letter of the law — in the hopes that

Congress and the state legislatures will not notice it is deceased, and future judges might someday declare that it still lives. Perhaps we should stop "explaining" the true meaning of the Second Amendment in the hopes that unbelievers may someday mistake its pallor for an unearthly beauty.

Perhaps it is time to recognize that we are an uncomfortably small minority with a tenuous hold on the remaining rights permitted us, and begin, with a bit more humility, rethinking how we will move beyond mere electoral, legislative and judicial stratagems to rekindling the spirit of the law among our fellow man. Lest circumstances someday overtake us and Americans re-learn the purpose and meaning of the Second Amendment the way people often re-learn the hard and bitter lessons of the past.

THE UNBEARABLE LIGHTNESS OF RIGHTS

If the government has the power to define what your rights are, do you really have any rights?

The Holy Grail of many gun rights activists is a Supreme Court ruling affirming that individuals have the right to keep and bear arms. This, it is supposed, will end oppressive anti-gun legislation, and calm the fears of gun owners that the government will confiscate their guns. But what if the desire for such a ruling were itself so wrong-headed as to undermine the right the ruling was supposed to proclaim?

The Second Amendment states, "A well-regulated militia, being necessary to the security of a free State, the right of the people to keep and bear arms, shall not be infringed." Note that this statement neither creates the right nor defines it. Instead, the statement refers to a pre-existent right long recognized by custom as a "natural" or God-given right belonging to the individual that is prior and superior to the Constitution itself.

These facts have serious implications. First, the source of authority of the rights of the people is superior to the Constitution. Second, if the Constitution does not create the right, and the right is superior to the Constitution itself, then the Constitution does not confer the authority to destroy or alter the right, for a lesser authority may not nullify or amend the act of a superior authority. Only the power which created the right has the authority to amend or abolish that right. Further, any law infringing the right is utterly without authority, and any judicial pronouncement on the meaning of the right which infringes the right is also without authority.

Since the right is not defined by the Constitution, the meaning and scope of the right is not within the province of the Constitution or the governmental entities created by the Constitution, including the courts. The scope of the right is determined independently by the historical tradition and customs that embody the right, not by an analysis of meaning of the words of the Second Amendment.

The upshot is that any "interpretation" of the right by the courts is not binding, either upon the people or the other branches of government. Since the right is neither a creation of positive law derived from the Constitution nor defined by the Constitution itself, the Court, itself a creation of the Constitution, cannot have supreme and final authority in this instance "to say what the law is" (as the Court described its authority in *Marbury v. Madison*). The Constitution, subordinate in authority to the people's rights, cannot confer a power upon the courts superior to or even co-equal with those rights. The Court's "interpretation" (which necessarily entails the risk of erroneous abridgement or expansion) of the people's rights therefore cannot be binding upon the people.

How, then, are our rights to be protected, if not by the Supreme Court? By ourselves. The right of trial by jury, wrested from King John in 1215 at sword-point and preserved in the Sixth Amendment, provides the daily, case by case means by which the people can guard their rights. As representative of the conscience of the community, the jury has the power to return a verdict of not guilty when the "law" violates these rights. The jury's power to nullify insures that the people retain guardianship of, and final authority over, their rights.

To view the Supreme Court as the guardian of your rights, to feel yourself bound by its pronouncements upon the existence or meaning of your rights, to crave these pronouncements as your true hope and salvation, is to slavishly accept the subjection of your rights to the political process. The Founders did not create a system of government in which you had to wait, either for the correct law or the correct judicial opinion, to possess your rights, because they preserved trial by jury.

Not everyone is likely to be convinced by these arguments (even assuming they contain no errors). Hard-boiled pragmatists may still cling to the hope for Supreme Court ruling because most people believe that the Court's rulings have final authority and "perception is reality." Let's take a look, then, at just what sort of protection the Supreme Court offers to individual rights these days, to see if this is really the road we want to travel.

The language of the Bill of Rights is categorical. For example, according to the First Amendment, Congress shall make *no law* abridging free speech. The Second Amendment states that the right to keep and bear arms *shall not be infringed*. Under the Fourth Amendment, the right of the people to be secure against unreasonable searches and seizures *shall not be violated*. This language contains no general exceptions or qualifications, such as, "unless justified by a compelling need," or "but only to the extent consistent with public safety."

To be sure, there is the question of defining the scope of these rights. A right means one thing, and not something else; it does not encompass all human behavior. So, for example, there may be a question whether the right to free speech or freedom of association really encompasses a right to give as much money as you want to the political candidate of your choice. So, too, there may be a question whether the right to keep and bear arms encompasses a right to own a tank. These questions may be particularly difficult to decide at the margins of the right. But if the particular behavior is determined to be within the scope of the right, then the language of the Bill of Rights is clear: the right shall not be abridged, infringed or violated.

137

This is not the view taken, however, by the Supreme Court. According to it, our rights are not absolute. Whether or not they are respected depends on a balancing test in which the right is weighed against the interests of the state that require an incursion upon the right. The right must yield if outweighed by a "compelling state interest." This is true for the right to free speech, freedom from unreasonable searches and seizures, the right to equal protection of the laws, and even for the newly minted right of abortion.

Examples of the Court's balancing approach are easy to find. In *Maryland v. Wilson* (1997 WL 65726), a case involving the question whether an officer making a traffic stop may order passengers to get out of the car while he completes his investigation and ticketing or arrest of the driver, the Court said "[t]he touchstone of our analysis under the Fourth Amendment is always 'the reasonableness in all the circumstances of the particular governmental invasion of a citizen's personal security,' . . . and that reasonableness 'depends on a balance between the public interest and the individual's right to personal security free from arbitrary interference by law officers'."

Similarly, in *Planned Parenthood of Southeastern PA v. Casey* (505 U.S. 833, 1992), in which the Supreme Court reconsidered the validity of *Roe v. Wade* and reaffirmed the woman's right to an abortion, the Court said "The woman's liberty is not so unlimited, however, that, from the outset, the State cannot show its concern for the life of the unborn and, at a later point in fetal development, the State's interest in life has sufficient force so that the right of the woman to terminate the pregnancy can be restricted. . . . viability . . . is the time at which there is a realistic possibility of maintaining a life outside the womb, so that the independent existence of the second life can, in reason and all fairness, be the object of state protection that now overrides the rights of the woman." (505 U.S. at p. 871; emphasis supplied).

Now to say that you may have your rights only so long as they are not outweighed by a compelling state interest is to assert that your rights exist only so long as they are, from the state's perspective, trivial, or at least, sufficiently unimportant. Yes, you may have your rights, as long as the state does not find it too restrictive or cumbersome to respect them.

The Court's faux, diversionary radicalism with "sexual rights" is a prime example of its largesse in matters which do not concern, or actually abet the growth of, state power. So the First Amendment protects topless dancing at the Kitty Kat lounge. Oooh, how radical! How un-bourgeois! What heady freedom! The Constitution protects my right to lose myself in sensual delights and pursue a life of sex without consequence! What a document! Just don't ask the federal government to eliminate the alphabet regulatory agencies that have no basis in the Constitution. Just don't ask it to stop regulating health, education and human welfare, for which it has no authority under the Constitution, or to eliminate the tax burden that results from this government overreaching. Just don't ask it to let you carry a hand-gun for protection without permission.

"But you go too far," you say. "Surely killing an unborn child is not trivial; the 'right' to abort a fetus is surely significant whether or not you believe it is a real right."[1] Sorry, not from the state's perspective, and it is the state's view that is determinative. The necessary legal implication of *Roe v. Wade* is that the fetus is not a "person" entitled to due process of law until it is born. From the state's perspective, the woman who aborts her fetus does not kill a "person;" it is not, therefore, a matter that seriously affects compelling or important state interests. From the state's perspective, in other words, the fetus is less than human, at least until viability. Cruelty to animal laws are more constitutionally enforceable than restrictions on abortions before viability.

The point of the "balancing test" is precisely to give final and ultimate weight to the state's authority. If rights were "absolute," there would be no question of weighing them against "interests" to determine when the rights must yield. The Court's balancing test gives the final and heaviest countervailing weight to the state.

---

1 For the record, the author does not believe that there is a right of abortion, and does believe that abortion is murder.

According to the Court, only the state's interests are ever "compelling."

How has the Court determined that the absolute, categorical prohibitions contained in the Bill of Rights actually permit violations when the state's need is "compelling"? Is it not surprising that a statement that *no* law shall be passed turns out to mean that *some* laws can be passed? How, according to the Court, do the categorical prohibitions in the Bill of Rights, which on their face appear to suggest that the conflicting interests of the state are to be given *no* account, turn out to actually *require* us to take the interests of the state into account and weigh them in the balance? Is this not surprising?

What legal or historical analysis has the Court made that explains why rights are, in fact, simply "weighty interests" that are required to be balanced against the weight of competing interests to determine whether they may be recognized? And more to the point, what source of authority confers the final, heaviest weight upon the interests of the state? Surely that is a question that requires an answer, especially since the categorical form of the prohibitions in the Bill of Rights suggests quite the opposite. I have not yet located answers to these questions in the Court's legal opinions, and suspect that they may not exist.

Well, but doesn't the qualification that rights are respected as long as the state's interest is not "compelling" still offer a large scope of individual freedom? Who can tell? How does one know when state interests are "compelling?" The Court offers no objective criteria for measuring the strength of state interests and, indeed, it would seem impossible to do so. The standard is quite vague and malleable. One could just as easily substitute the following words for "compelling" in the Court's opinions with absolutely no loss of meaning and no change in result: a right must yield to the interests of the state if that interest "seems to us, at the time and under the circumstances, really, really important." Or these words will work equally well: the right may be set aside "if it seems like a really good idea at the time" (much as, for example, the internment of Japenese-Americans during World War II). In short, the "compelling" standard must be a lot like obscenity: the Court cannot define it, but it knows it when it sees it.

And the consequence of this is: no one can know what his rights are until after the fact, that is, until after the Court has weighed the competing interests in each particular set of facts and circumstances and pronounced whether or not the right must be respected in those circumstances. Let me say that again: the consequence of the Court's philosophy that the degree of respect accorded to rights depends on a weighing of competing interests under the particular facts and circumstances is that you cannot know what your rights are until the government tells you what they are, something that can be known only after the fact.

Nor is the "balancing test" the only means by which the Court has built elbow room and flexibility into the categorical prohibitions of the Bill of Rights. Another method, particularly evident in the Court's Fourth Amendment jurisprudence, is to interpret and apply the amendment in light of its purpose instead of adhering to the actual, literal words of the amendment.

The modern Court has discovered that the purpose of the Fourth Amendment is to protect people's "reasonable expectations of privacy" and so this has become the Court's standard for determining how far law enforcement can go in conducting searches and seizures. Yes, true, the Fourth Amendment doesn't actually say anything like that, nor can we find such 20th Century psychobabble in any of the writings of the Founding Fathers, but this criticism just shows how unfit we are to be Supreme Court justices.

Now, because people's expectations of privacy vary in different circumstances, the Court has concluded that our Fourth Amendment rights similarly vary. So, case law now proclaims your rights are stronger in your home than when you are in your car. They are better if you own than if you rent. They are better if you build a solid privacy fence around your yard than if you put up a chain link fence. Your rights are stronger if you are a passenger in a car than if you are the driver. Personal papers like letters and diaries are more protected than business records, etc. A different Fourth Amendment rule for every occasion!

Pray, tell, how does the Court know what our "expectations of privacy" are? Is it necessary, when bringing a Fourth Amendment case, to commission a Zogby poll to determine the American populace's expectations of privacy to prove your case to the Court? Is this factual information part of the record of the case? Does the Court independently commission its own poll, or do other sociological research to determine what our expectations are?

No! No! That is the beauty of it. The justices need consult only their own minds and experience. They simply apply the skills of textual exegesis they use every day in examining cases and statutes to life itself. The interior of cars are exposed to common view because the car travels on public property and has unobstructed windows. Therefore, people have less expectation of privacy than they do in their own homes. That sort of thing.

And then, the analysis is not principally factual but legal: what expectations are "reasonable" for people to have in the circumstances, regardless of whether or not the majority, or even anyone, actually feels that way? Thus, the Court's Fourth Amendment opinions often contain statements hypothesizing about how people being subjected to a particular form of search or seizure *should* feel about what is happening to them.

And the consequences are, not only are there an innumerable number of variations in your Fourth Amendment rights, which, like clothing, vary to suit the occasion, but again you cannot know what your rights are until after the fact, when the Court has informed you what is reasonable for you to expect in the circumstances.

Rights which are forfeit if the government's need to infringe them is "compelling," rights which vary in strength depending on the degree to which they achieve the "purpose" of the right in the circumstances, these are the sort of blessings we will inherit if the Supreme Court ever deigns to recognize the Second Amendment. And if your reaction is, well, this just shows that we need to place better people on the bench who not only will recognize the Second Amendment, but adhere to a proper understanding of the Bill of Rights as a whole, then you surely miss the point.

To believe this, to act on this basis, is to concede that your rights depend on what the Court says, and are subject to the political process of election and appointment, i.e., majority or plurality rule. The Year 2000 election battle between candidates Bush and Gore provides proof positive of this point. We are told this election is critical and that we must vote, for the next President will be able to appoint three or four justices to the Supreme Court. In other words, the majority, the political process will decide the future of your rights.

Do you really think that the Founding Fathers, who believed that our rights came from God, created a system of government in which your rights depended upon the opinion of man - majority rule and 5 of 9 Supreme Court justices?

So I ask again: If government has the power to define your rights, do you really have any rights? No. If you look to the government to recognize and enforce your rights, then you will only have such rights as the government will acknowledge.

Individual rights are yours, they are in your possession, but they live only if you live them, by acting upon them without let or leave from government, and by nullifying laws that violate those rights in your capacity as a juror. They require no positive act of government to make them real or meaningful, or to "protect" them, because in each instance all that they require of government is that it leave you alone, that government do *nothing*.

Ignore the state's claims to an authority that it cannot possess. Do not vest in it any power, real or imagined, to proclaim or protect the rights recognized in the Bill of Rights. The government has no authority over those rights; therefore, do not ask it to exercise any and do not act as if it does. Your rights are your responsibility. If you believe for one minute that you must wait until the government recognizes your rights before you may act on them, whether by court opinion or legislation such as concealed carry reform, then *you* have abandoned your rights.

WALTER MITTY'S SECOND AMENDMENT

Once upon a time, there was a people who inhabited a majestic land under an all powerful government. Now this government had the resources to control practically every aspect of human existence; hundreds of thousands of "public servants" could access the most personal details about every citizen because each citizen was issued a number at birth with which the government could track him throughout his life. No one could even work in gainful employment without this number.

True, the government left certain domains of individual action largely free, particularly matters concerning speech and sex. But these activities posed no real threat to the state. When not used to entertain and divert, the power of speech was used principally to clamor for more or better goods from the state, or for "reforms" to make the state work "better," thereby entrenching the people's dependency. And insofar as sex was concerned, well, the people's behavior in this area also really had no effect on the scope of state power.

In fact, the rulers noted that people's preoccupation with sex and sexual morality — whether premarital, teenage pregnancy, adultery, divorce, homosexuality or general "who's zooming who"

— diverted the people's attention from the fact that they were, for economic and all other intents and purposes, slaves. Slaves, though, who labored under the illusion that they were free. The people were a simple lot, politically speaking, and readily mistook the ability to give free reign to their appetites as the essence of "personal freedom."

In that fruitful land, the state took about 50 percent of everything the people earned through numerous forms of taxation, up from about 25 percent only a generation earlier. However, this boastful people, who believed themselves to be the freest on earth, retained the right to keep and bear arms. Tens of millions possessed firearms, *just in case* their government ever became tyrannical, and enslaved them.

In that land, countless regulations, filling more than 100,000 pages in the state's "code of regulations," were promulgated by persons who were not elected by the people. The regulators often developed close relationships with the businesses they regulated, and worked in "agencies" that had the power both to make law — and to enforce it. The agencies were not established by the government's constitution, and their existence violated that instrument's principle of separation of powers. Yet the people retained the right to keep and bear arms. *Just in case* their government, *some day*, ceased to be a "government of the people."

The country's constitution contemplated that the people would be governed by two levels of government — "national" and "local." Matters that concerned people most intimately — health, education, welfare, crime and the environment — were to be left almost exclusively to local government, so that those who made and enforced the laws lived close to the people who were subject to the laws, and felt their effects. So that different people who had different ideas about such things would not be subject to a "one size fits all" standard that would apply if the national government dealt with these matters. Competition among different localities for people, who could move freely from one place to another, would act as a "reality check" on the passage of unnecessary or unwise laws.

But in a time of great crisis called the Great Economic Downturn, the people and their leaders clamored for "national solutions to national problems," and the constitution was "interpreted" by the Majestic Court to permit the national government to pass laws regulating practically everything that had been reserved to the localities. Now the people had the pleasure of being governed by not one but two beneficent governments with two sets of laws regulating the same things. Now the people could be prosecuted by not one but two governments for the same activities and conduct.

Still this fiercely independent people retained the right to keep and bear arms. Just in case their government, some day, no longer secured the blessings of liberty to themselves and their posterity.

In that fair land, a property owner could be held liable under the nation's environmental legislation for the clean-up costs associated with toxic chemicals, even if the owner had not caused the problem. Another set of laws provided for asset forfeiture, and permitted government agencies to confiscate property without first establishing guilt. Yet the people retained the right to keep and bear arms. Just in case their government denied them due process by holding them liable for things that were not their fault.

(The Majestic Court had long ago determined that "due process" did not prevent government from imposing liability on people who were not at fault. "Due process," it turned out, meant little more than that a law had been passed, or a regulation promulgated, in accordance with the established procedures. You know, it was actually voted on, passed by a majority and signed by the President. If it met those standards, it didn't matter what the law actually *did*.)

Oh well, the people had little real cause to worry. After all, those laws hardly ever affected anyone that anyone knew. Certainly not the people who mattered most of all: the country's favorite celebrities and sports teams, who so occupied the people's attention. And how bad could it be if it had not yet been the subject of a Movie Of The Week, telling them what to think and how to feel about it?

In that wide open land, the police often established roadblocks to check that the people's papers were in order, and used these occasions to ask the occupants whether they were carrying weapons or drugs. Sometimes the police would ask to search the vehicles, and the occupants — not knowing whether they could say no and wanting to prove their good faith by cooperating — would permit it. The Majestic Court had pronounced these roadblocks and searches lawful, on the novel theory, unknown to the country's Founding Forebears, that so long as the police were doing this to everyone equally, it didn't violate anyone's rights in particular.

The roadblocks sometimes caused annoying delays, but these lovers of the open road took it in stride. After all, they retained the right to keep and bear arms. Just in case their government, some day, engaged in unreasonable searches and seizures.

In that bustling land, the choice of how to develop property was not left to the owner, but was heavily regulated by local governments that often demanded fees or concessions for the privilege. That is, when the development was not prohibited outright by national "moistland" regulations that had no foundation in statutory or constitutional law. Even home owners often required permission simply to build an addition to their homes, or to erect a tool shed on their so-called private property. And so it seemed that "private property" became, not a system protecting individual liberty, but a system which, while providing the illusion of ownership, actually just allocated and assigned government-mandated burdens and responsibilities.

Still, this mightily productive people believed themselves to live in the most capitalistic society on earth, a society dedicated to the protection of private property. And so they retained the right to keep and bear arms. Just in case their government ever sought to deprive them of their property without just compensation.

Besides, the people had little cause for alarm. Far from worrying about government control of their property, the more immediate problem was what to buy next! The people were a simple lot, politically speaking, and readily mistook the ability to acquire an endless assortment of consumer goods as the essence of personal freedom.

The enlightened rulers of this great land did not seek to deprive the people of their right to arms. Unlike tyrants of the past, they had learned that it was not necessary. The people proved time and again to be willing accomplices to the ever expanding authority of government, enslaved by their own desire for safety, security and welfare. The people could have their guns. What did the rulers care? They already possessed the complete obedience that they required.

In fact, in their more Machiavellian moments, the rulers could be heard to admit that permitting the people the right to keep and bear arms was a marvelous tool of social control, for it provided the people with the illusion of freedom. The people, among the most highly regulated on earth, told themselves that they were free because they retained the means of revolt. Just in case things ever got really bad. No one, however, seemed to have too clear an idea what "really bad" really meant. The people accepted the fact that their government no longer even remotely resembled the plan set forth in their original constitution. And the people's values no longer remotely resembled those of their Founding Forebears.

Yet in their naivete, how fiercely the people clung to this illusion! As if the "means of revolt" were to be found in a piece of inanimate metal! Really it was laughable, and pathetic.

No, the rulers knew that the people could safely be trusted with arms. The government educated their children, it provided for retirement in their old age, bequeathed assistance if they lost their jobs, mandated that they receive health care and doled out food and shelter if they were poor.

The government was the very air the people breathed from childhood to the grave, and few could imagine, let alone desire, any other kind of world. To the extent that they paid any attention to their system of government, the great mass spent their days simply clamoring for more or better "programs," more "rational" regulations, in short, more of the same. The only thing that really upset them was waste, fraud or abuse in the existing programs, which sometimes triggered vehement protests demanding that government provide their services more efficiently!

The nation's stirring national anthem, adopted long ago by men who fought for their liberty, ended by posing a question, in hopes of keeping the spirit of liberty alive. Did the flag still fly, it asked, over the land of the free? Unfortunately, few considered that the answer to that question might really be no, for they had long since lost an understanding of what freedom is.

No, in this land "freedom" had become something dark, frightening and dangerous. The people lived in mortal terror that somewhere, sometime, some individual might make a decision or embark upon a course of action that was not first approved by some government official. Security was far preferable, for how could anyone be truly free, if he were not first absolutely safe and protected?

Now we must say goodbye to this fair country whose government toiled tirelessly to create the safety, fairness and luxury that all demanded, and that everyone knew could be created by passing just the right laws. Through it all, the people vigorously safeguarded their tradition of firearms ownership. But they never knew — and never learned — that preserving a tradition and a way of life is not the same as preserving liberty. And they never knew — and never learned — that it's not about guns.

REVOLUTION

"But when a long Train of Abuses and Usurpations, pursuing invariably the same Object, evinces a Design to reduce them under absolute Despotism, it is their Right, it is their Duty, to throw off such Government, and to provide new Guards for their future Security."

The Declaration of Independence

THE LINE IN THE SAND

There can be no doubt that 1994 marks the turning point for the right to keep and bear arms in America. The Brady Act, the assault weapons ban, and proposed laws now before Congress to require national registration of firearms, licensing of gun owners, imposition of new taxes on guns and ammunition and higher license fees for firearms' dealers, make it quite clear that keeping and bearing arms is now regarded by both the executive and legislative branches of the federal government, and by both Democrats and Republicans, as a mere privilege, utterly subject to condition and qualification imposed by law, and that gun ownership is an evil to be curbed.

At each turn these laws have been presented as reasonable, moderate precautions to insure society's safety, to protect us and our children, from violent crime. At each turn, proponents of the law promise that these laws will protect us by preventing crime, by keeping guns out of the wrong hands.

The siren song of promised safety is seductive, and has lured many gun owners to support these measures. But are these laws simply "reasonable" precautions that do not undermine the right to keep and bear arms? Let's briefly consider the operating principles of these laws.

The Brady Bill

While many gun owners view Brady as a relatively harmless nuisance and others believe background checks a sound idea, it is hard to underestimate the significance of this law: Brady deprives firearms purchasers of the presumption of innocence, and requires them to prove, to the government's satisfaction, that they are worthy of owning a firearm.

It is illegal to sell a firearm to a felon. To prevent this, we passed a law the intent of which is to treat everyone who wants to acquire a gun as ineligible, i.e., effectively presuming that every purchaser is a felon, until information in the hands and control of the government proves that he is not. Should the information in the hands of the government be wrong, the prospective purchaser bears the burden of proving his innocence, i.e., that he is not a felon and is eligible to acquire a gun.

Having established the principle that gun ownership is conditioned upon prior proof, to the government's satisfaction, of eligibility to own a firearm, and that those who want firearms are not entitled to the presumption of innocence, Brady holds real potential as a tool of disarmament through expansion of the list of disqualifying criteria. After all, since persons who want firearms are unworthy of the presumption of innocence and bear the burden of proving that they are not a menace to society, there is no logical reason why these criteria should not be expanded as seems necessary to insure the public's safety.

Assault weapons

The assault weapon ban prohibits the manufacture, other than for sale to the military or law enforcement, of 19 specific semiautomatic weapons, and any other semiautomatic firearm that has a detachable magazine and at least two of a set of characteristics generally found on military or law enforcement weapons, such as pistol grips, folding stocks or bayonet lugs. The new law also lists, as specifically not subject to the ban, over 650 sporting rifles and shotguns.

As an attempt to control crime, the ban is laughable. By all accounts, these guns are used in less than 1 percent of all gun crime, and the outlawed, evil characteristics have no relationship whatsoever to gun crime. There are no known cases of inner-city gang warfare by bayonet charge.

The facts that the law prohibits the acquisition of these firearms by the law-abiding, outlaws military features, and purports to protect "sporting" weapons, drives home the main purpose of the law: to establish the principle that the only legitimate reason that the law-abiding may own firearms is for "sporting purposes."

Recent legal and historical scholarship, such as Joyce Malcolm's book, *To Keep and Bear Arms—The Origins of an Anglo-American Right* (Harvard University Press), clearly establishes that the purpose of the Second Amendment was precisely to insure that individuals had the right to keep and bear firearms suitable to militia use, for our nation was founded upon the belief that a citizen militia— not a standing army, not a police force— was "necessary to the security of a free state."

Among the firearms specifically prohibited by the assault weapon ban is the Colt AR-15, the semiautomatic version of our military's basic firearm. By outlawing militia weapons, by establishing the principle that citizens may own only "sporting weapons," the assault weapon ban guts the Second Amendment.[1]

Dangerous questions

The Second Amendment was not intended to insure the avail-

---

1. In the last Supreme Court case to consider the Second Amendment, *U.S. v. Miller* (307 U.S. 174, 1939), the Supreme Court upheld the conviction of Miller, a moonshiner, for possession of an unregistered short-barreled (sawed-off) shotgun in violation of the registration and tax provisions of the National Firearms Act of 1934. The Court stated that in the absence of any evidence in the record before it that Miller's sawed-off shotgun "at this time has some reasonable relationship to the preservation or efficiency of a well regulated militia" (Ibid., at 177), the Court could not sustain Miller's contention that his possession of the weapon was protected by the Second Amendment. The implication from this statement is that individuals have a right to possess precisely those weapons which "at this time" have a reasonable relationship to the preservation of a militia. In today's context, that means the fully automatic M-16, the basic service weapon of the Army.

ability of a source of pleasant pastimes and diversions. It is the ultimate warrant that government governs only with the consent of the governed, the final surety and certain acknowledgment that government is the servant of the people, not their master. Violation of the Second Amendment is a denial both of the sovereignty of the people and the inalienable right of each person to life, by deprivation of the most effective means for exercising and protecting that right.

Seeing our government's encroachments upon the right to keep and bear arms, seeing, further, that those encroachments rest upon an utter denial of the existence of the right, those not lured by the siren song of promised safety are afraid that our government may be degenerating into tyranny. And some have begun to ask hard and dangerous questions.

When are people morally justified in violating or resisting, by any and all appropriate means, the duly enacted laws of their country? When has the very government — and not just this or that particular law — become tyrannical and illegitimate? When are people morally justified to take up arms against their government?

The strategy and plain intent of gun control proponents is to relentlessly whittle away the right to keep and bear arms, always avoiding outright confiscation but erecting barriers to the future ownership or use of firearms, so that the right will atrophy and die.

The 1986 machine gun ban, and the assault weapon ban, for example, do not confiscate or outlaw the existing stock of such firearms, but ban their future sale. Licensing requirements to own firearms or purchase ammunition and proposed tax increases would not affect firearms' owners existing stock, but would erect significant administrative and cost hurdles to the continued enjoyment of firearms and impose practical limits on the extent to which firearms were available or usable.

Each successive measure is lauded by gun-gun control proponents as but "a good first step." Seeing this, it is apparent that if we sit idly by, or fight through the ballot box and yet lose battle after battle in the legislature to an anti-gun majority, and lose battle after battle in courts refusing, whether willfully or ignorantly, to uphold the Second Amendment, the right will be gone.

Some fear that, if the right to keep and bear arms is to be not only preserved, but fully restored, the time may come when we shall have no recourse but to fight for our rights, with arms. So some seek a sign — to draw a line in the sand to warn our legislature and our opponents to go no further, a line which, if crossed, would signify to one and all that our government had gone too far, and that, as Patrick Henry said in urging Virginia to war against the British, "... an appeal to arms and the God of Hosts is all that is left us."

Madmen and malcontents

The questions many are now asking regarding the limits of allegiance to the state are among the most difficult moral and philosophical questions man has asked, and admit of no easy or precise answer. Our own history and heritage, however, do provide forceful answers to these questions. And though we will see that it does not draw the bright line we seek to help us distinguish between tyranny and legitimate government, let alone set the trigger point for armed insurrection, perhaps we will yet find it offers us some instruction.

Few political philosophers were as influential in shaping the American system of government as John Locke. In *The Second Treatise on Government* (1690), Locke defined tyranny as "the exercise of power beyond right."[2] Asking when the law might justly be opposed by force, he answered that "... *force* is to be opposed to nothing, but to unjust and unlawful *force*; whoever makes any opposition in any other case, draws on himself a just condemnation both from God and man." *[Emphasis in original]* [3] He further qualified this with the condition that force may justly be used to

---

2 John Locke, *Second Treatise of Government*, edited by C.B. Macpherson, Hackett Publishing Company, Inc., publisher, at Chapter 18,¶ 199, p. 101.
3 Ibid., at ¶204, p.103.

oppose the unlawful exercise of power only when there is no occasion for seeking a remedy through lawful means, for example, through the courts, or through petition of the legislature for redress of grievances:

> "For where the injured party may be relieved, and his damages repaired by appeal to the law, there can be no pretense for force, which is only to be used where a man is intercepted from appealing to the law; for nothing is to be accounted hostile force, but when it leaves not the remedy of such an appeal; and it is such *force* alone, that puts him that uses it *into a state of war*, and makes it lawful to resist him." [Emphasis in original][4]

If, however, the same unlawful exercise of power also precludes or obstructs a remedy through lawful means, then the person subjected to such "manifests act of tyranny" has the right to resist. Yet, Locke points out, though persons in such circumstances have the right to resist, their exercise of that right will not "disturb the government" if the government's exercise of unlawful power be perceived by the people at large as merely affecting only "some men's private cases." Moreover, many who are subject to tyranny in such circumstances will not avail themselves of this right to resist, because it would be pointless or suicidal:

> "For if [tyranny] reach no farther than some private men's cases, though they have a right to defend themselves, and to recover by force what by unlawful force is taken from them; yet the right to do so will not easily engage them in a contest, wherein they are sure to perish; it being as impossible for one, or a few oppressed men to *disturb the government*, where the body of the people do not think themselves concerned in it, as for a raving mad-man, or heady malcontent to overturn a well-settled state; the people being as little apt to follow the one, as the other." [Emphasis in original][5]

---

4 Ibid., at ¶207, p.105.
5 Ibid., at ¶208, pp.105-106

Armed resistance becomes probable and the government becomes susceptible to overthrow and revolution only when "a long train of abuses" make the government's tyrannical design visible to the people at large:

> "But if either these illegal acts have extended to the majority of the people; or if the mischief and oppression has lighted only on some few, but in such cases, as the precedent, and consequences seem to threaten all; and they are persuaded in their consciences that their laws, and with them their estates, liberties, and lives are in danger, and perhaps their religion too; . . . . But if a long train of abuses, prevarications and artifices, all tending the same way, make the design visible to the people, and they cannot but feel what they lie under, and see whither they are going; it is not to be wondered, that they should then rouse themselves, and endeavor to put the rule into such hands which may secure to them the ends for which government was at first erected."[6]

Consent of the governed

From Locke, we might draw two important lessons regarding resistance to our government's exercise of power beyond the right of the people to keep and bear arms. First, though people be justified in resisting tyranny, they are justified in using force only in self-defense. Force may not be used aggressively, to coerce a change in the government of the law. Though Locke does not directly elaborate on the reasons for this, we may. Governments derive their just powers only from the consent of the governed. Consent ends where force begins. A change in the government or in the law effected by force — rather than the free consent of the governed — is forever illegitimate.

There are, of course, many non-violent means of resistance to unjust or immoral laws, from simple non-compliance to active violation. Our own history furnishes examples of these. Long before the Civil War brought an end to slavery, for example, a small but

---

6 Ibid., at ¶209, p.106, and Chapter 19, ¶225, at p. 113.

dedicated group of people ran an "underground railway" to free slaves, in manifest violation of the Fugitive Slave Act and various state laws. Rosa Parks did not wait for the government's permission to sit in the front of the bus.

It behooves all who believe there is a higher authority than the state to contemplate their example.

Secondly, Locke teaches this: though we would be morally justified in resistance to tyrannical laws in violation of the Second Amendment by non-compliance (i.e., refusal to register our firearms), active violation (e.g., underground manufacture and sale of prohibited magazines) or, ultimately, under circumstances in which lethal force would be justified solely in defense of our lives, by force of arms, yet as long as our resistance is perceived merely as the efforts of a group of hobbyists and sportsmen angered over the loss of their deadly toys —— as our opponents consistently portray it —— our government's exercise of power beyond its right —— tyranny —— will be seen to "reach no farther than some men's private cases," and will not "disturb the government."

Though we may be morally justified in using force to defend ourselves against, for example, government use of force of arms to confiscate our firearms, if the body of the people do not see themselves concerned in it, our resistance will be seen as no better than the actions of madmen or malcontents. Moreover, in such circumstances, few would be willing to have recourse to the right to resist, as they would merely be engaging in "a contest wherein [they were] sure to perish."

Consider, as a modern-day proof of the truth of Locke's observation to the American people's non-reaction to the federal government's behavior at Waco. Insist as they might that they acted only in self-defense and upon principled opposition to unlawful behavior by the United States government, the Branch Davidians were regarded as no better than "madmen or heady malcontents." Ultimately, their defiant stance did not in the least "disturb the government," not even to the extent of forcing the resignation of

Attorney General Reno, who in fact received plaudits from the media for "accepting responsibility" for her "errors in judgment."

If resistance to gun-control laws is based on guns, or the enjoyment of guns, rather than our inalienable right to life and the sovereignty of the people, if we are consistently perceived as concerned only that we be left undisturbed to enjoy target shooting, hunting or collecting fine firearms, if, in fact, that is all that we do care about, then resistance by an angry few will likely prove futile, and we will lose — not secure — the right to keep and bear arms.

Self-government, not war

Though he did not live to see it, Locke's political principles regarding the dissolution of government found concrete expression in American history. When our Founding Fathers had had enough of English government, they fearlessly and formally announced, in the Declaration of Independence, that they no longer regarded themselves subject to the King of England or the laws of Parliament.

They began by asserting, as self-evident truths, that governments are instituted to secure our inalienable rights, among them, life, liberty and the pursuit of happiness, and derive their just powers only from the consent of the governed; that whenever any form of government becomes destructive of these ends, it is the right of the people to alter or to abolish it, and to institute a new government.

The Declaration then establishes that Locke's criteria justifying exercise of the people's right to abolish a tyrannical government had been satisfied:

"Prudence, indeed, will dictate that Governments long established should not be changed for light and transient Causes; and accordingly all Experience hath shewn, that Mankind are more disposed to suffer, while Evils are sufferable, than to right themselves by abolishing the Forms to which they are accustomed. *But when a long Train of*

161

Abuses and Usurpations, pursuing invariably the same Object, evinces a Design to reduce them under absolute Despotism, it is their Right, it is their Duty, to throw off such Government, and to provide new Guards for their future Security."
[Emphasis supplied]

The Declaration makes a lengthy list of the "long Train of Abuses and Usurpations" by England evincing a design to reduce the colonies under absolute despotism. But even this long train of abuses was not sufficient. We had also exhausted the means for rectifying these abuses, by petitioning Crown and Parliament, and by appeals to the common interest, humanity and sense of justice of the people of England, and understood that further appeals would be useless:

"In every stage of these Oppressions We have Petitioned for Redress in the most humble terms: Our repeated Petitions have been answered only by repeated Injury... Nor have We been wanting in attention to our British Brethren. We have warned them from time to time of attempts by their Legislature to extend an unwarrantable Jurisdiction over us. . . . We have appealed to their native Justice and Magnanimity, and we have conjured them by Ties of our common Kindred to disavow these Usurpations. . . . They, too, have been deaf to the Voice of Justice and Consanguinity. We must, therefore, acquiesce in the Necessity which denounces our Separation, and hold them, as we hold the rest of Mankind, Enemies in War, in Peace, Friends."

Though the Declaration recapitulates Locke's criteria for the dissolution of a government, its significance is not fully appreciated without considering what that document did *not* say or do. We did *not* declare war on England; we declared that by its deeds England's governance over us had rendered itself illegitimate, and that we were, therefore, free of any allegiance to it. We did *not* set out to punish or avenge, with force of arms, the misdeeds against us; we simply declared that *we would now govern ourselves*. To be sure, war would follow, for it was not to be expected that England would give up the colonies without a fight. Yet war was not our intent; *our intent was to govern ourselves.*

By recognizing the tyrannical nature of English governance and publicly declaring it illegitimate, any use of force of arms by England against us under pretense of lawful authority now became a naked act of aggression, and our resistance to it became moral and just self-defense.

French Revolution

The American Revolution has always been profitably contrasted with the French Revolution. Unlike the American Revolution, the French Revolution began with an assault on the most hated and dread symbol of the French people's oppression, the Bastille, and was driven by desperate desire and need to tear down the *ancien regime.*

Unlike our ancestors' problems with Britain, the problems of the French people inhered not just in their government, but in the very structure of French society. The blood-bath, utter anarchy and madness that followed was, for a long, dark time, no more than the settling of old scores, retribution for long-standing, horrible wrongs, a purge of the ruling class and those too closely associated with it and its interests, which even those at the helm of the revolutionary government could not control.

That was not our beginning. the Declaration of Independence teaches us that resistance by the people to their government is not just, nor will it be justly waged, unless born of the commitment to govern themselves. This is an important point, for there is much evidence that our predicament is in great measure due precisely to the American people's rejection of self-government.

We have met the enemy

Consider that our predicament may be worse than that of our ancestors, that, subject to a remote government, lacking the rights to representation in Parliament, it was, perhaps, easier for them to come to the painful conclusion to separate from England.

163

Consider that our difficulties lie along a different path: that our government represents us *too* well.

Do the Brady Act and the assault weapon ban violate the Constitution? Have our legislators and president violated their oath of office in voting for this legislation? Certainly. But anger at this betrayal should not cloud our sight of a more disturbing reality: this is what the American people *want*. Polls indicated that approximately 70 percent of American people supported the assault weapon ban.

We have met the enemy, and it is us.

Now if our difficulties lie in the character of the American people at large, if we have the government we deserve, then the notion that armed resistance to the government is any kind of means to restoring the rights intended to be preserved by our Founding Fathers is utterly misguided. In fact, if our difficulties lie principally in the character of the American people rather than in our government *per se*, then our situation is not analogous to that of our ancestors in the years preceding the American Revolution, but is closer to that of the French, whose problems were deeply rooted in the structure of their society. This possibility should give great pause to anyone glibly ready to declare war on government officials.

The passage of the assault weapon ban reveals a painful truth which we would do well to recognize. Seventy percent of the American people — and obviously a sizable percentage of gun owners — accept the notion that no one should own a "weapon of war whose sole purpose is to kill people" which has "no legitimate sporting purpose." Yet the fact that no one seeks to deny the use of "assault weapons" by the police or federal law enforcement indicates that, despite the rhetoric about "weapons of war," people truly understand that these firearms are not evil in themselves, and have obvious utility for defense of home, community and nation.

And since people know this, but believe that it is right to confine their ownership of firearms to those suitable only for "sporting purposes," the real significance of the assault weapon ban is that the great majority of Americans disavow any serious responsibility to protect themselves or their communities from violent crime or civil unrest, and fully expect this to be done for them, by the state.

The assault weapon ban illustrates how we lose our freedoms, namely, by our refusal to assume the responsibilities of self-government. If the citizens will not form a militia for their own protection and collectively assume the burden of policing their streets, defending their communities from riot or civil unrest or their country from foreign invasion, as was the case at our founding, but will push off that responsibility to a separate, select police force and a separate, select standing army, then those owning firearms are left with no legitimate, non-frivolous reasons for having weapons.

Frivolous reasons

Since most Americans have renounced the responsibility for which firearms are needed and shifted this duty entirely to government, they cannot believe, and will not take seriously, claims by others, in the minority, that the firearms are needed for serious purposes. In the view of the majority, those continuing to own firearms do so only for two remaining reasons: either they harbor dangerous, illegitimate intentions (i.e., they intend to commit crimes), or they harbor legitimate but utterly frivolous ones: hunting, recreation, competitive shooting, collecting.

Since most Americans have renounced the responsibility for which firearms are needed, they will not presume or believe that those owning firearms are motivated or controlled by considerations of responsibility. They will readily accept, therefore, the necessity of laws to insure that firearms owners will behave and act safely, and do not harbor dangerous intentions.

The rejection of the burdens of self-government — in this case the responsibility to defend our lives and our communities from violent crime and civil unrest — and the attempt to place the principal responsibility for that duty upon the institutions of government, thus leads inexorably to the destruction of the rights which exist only to insure the freedom of those willing to govern themselves. Gun owners are often as guilty of this as those who seek to deprive them of their right to keep arms.

Every time we insist that the answer to violent crime lies in more police, more prisons, no parole, stiffer penalties and longer sentences, or more poverty, drug treatment or Head Start programs, every time, in short, we suggest that with a few needed reforms and programs, our institutions would be fully up to the task of reducing violent crime to minor levels, so that we citizens need no longer worry about violent crime, we implicitly renounce any personal responsibility for crime in our communities and declare that we lack any serious reason for owning firearms, and thereby drive another nail in the coffin of the Second Amendment.

What is to be done?

Isaac Asimov, in his *Foundation* trilogy, had a character once say, "Violence is the last refuge of the incompetent." Asimov was a very intelligent man, and perhaps he, or his character, believed that there was no political problem that did not, through the application of superior intelligence, admit of a non-violent solution. Whether this be true may be difficult to say, but it is clear in any event that violence is the first, second or third refuge of the incompetent.

Talk of gun owners engaging in armed insurrection against their government to rescue their Second Amendment rights indicates, at this point, that we have utterly failed to identify the source of our problems. Our forefathers, engaged in building a nation in the wilderness, were a free and independent people, who keenly felt and resented a distant and unrepresentative government's attempts to restrict their liberty and exploit their labors. Modern Americans, in contrast, for the most part are, and crave to be, completely dependent upon government, wanting nothing better than to reform their government and give it enough power so that it will, at last, really work, properly educating their children, protecting them from violent crime, seeing to it that they are provided food, shelter and health care, a comfortable retirement, et cetera.

There is a line in the sand that distinguishes between legitimate and tyrannical government, and it was drawn by the Founding Fathers. It is called the United States Constitution. It is breached every day, and has been for a long, long time now. It is and was breached because our legislators and courts have given us — not always, not completely or perfectly, but basically — what we, the American people, have asked for.

Locke teaches us that a tyrannical government will be dissolved only when a long train of abuses makes evident to the people at large its design to reduce them under utter despotism. Since a just government governs only with the consent of the government, a tyrannical government is not justly dissolved and replaced until a sizable enough percentage of the governed recognize its tyrannical nature, and institute a new government upon principles they believe will secure their liberties.

Gun owners who are serious about preserving their rights must become politically active in the way in which our Founding Fathers were politically active. It is not enough to vote, contact representatives, donate funds or even run for office. We must study again the Declaration of Independence, our Constitution and the Federalist Papers, and judge where we are today against where the Founding Fathers hoped we would be. We must read the classics of political philosophy, and question the nature, purpose and limits of government, and consider what principles and institutional structures might best secure liberty, and limit government to the ends for which it is instituted, thinking always of what our Founding Fathers attempted and questioning where they — or we — may have failed.

If we perceive tyranny in our government's attempts to deprive us of the right to arms, then rather than rushing to join Locke's madmen and heady malcontents in an ineffective, suicidal declaration of war on government, we need to do the hard work of educating ourselves and others, and forging relationships with those who perceive the government's "Abuses and Usurpations" in other arenas. The new Committees of Correspondence may be found on talk radio, the Internet, and in organizations like the Cato Institute and the Federalist Society.

Our efforts will bear fruit, however, only if we proceed on but one basis. If we wish to reclaim our rights, we must begin by reclaiming our responsibilities. If we wish to secure the blessings of liberty to ourselves and our posterity, we must begin by declaring that *now we will govern ourselves*. For with responsibility comes freedom.

ACKNOWLEDGEMENTS

"A Nation of Cowards" appeared originally in *The Public Interest*, Number 113, Fall, 1993. It is reprinted here with the permission of National Affairs, Inc.

"A License to Save Your Life" appeared originally in *The Washington Times*, January 20, 1994, page A17. Copyright ©1994 News World Communications, Inc. Reprinted with permission of The Washington Times.

"Guns and Feminism" appeared originally as "Feminist Magazine Urges Women to Reject Guns for Self-Defense" in *American Handgunner*, September/October 1994. It is reprinted here courtesy of Publishers Development Corporation.

"Who's Under Assault in the Assault Weapon Ban?" appeared originally in *The Washington Times*, August 25, 1994, page A19. Copyright ©1994 News World Communications, Inc. Reprinted with permission of The Washington Times.

"Fighting Crime with Crime" is a reworked version of articles appearing originally as "Past 20 Years Have Seen Worst Gun Control Gains This Century" and "Is It Better to Be Safe or Free? in the September/October 1996 and November/December 1996 issues of *American Handgunner.* It is reprinted here courtesy of Publishers Development Corporation.

"Guns and Schools" appeared originally as "Gun-Free School Zone Act Based on Fallacious Premise of Laws" in *American Handgunner,* March/April 1997. It is reprinted here courtesy of Publishers Development Corporation.

"Teach Your Children Well" appeared originally as "'Zero Tolerance' Policies Defy Morality and Rush to Conformity" in *American Handgunner,* May/June 1998. It is reprinted here courtesy of Publishers Development Corporation.

"You're Doing This Because of the Numbers?" appeared originally as "Studies That 'Prove' Guns Are Good Or Bad Are Equally Wrong" in *American Handgunner,* January/February 1995. It is reprinted here courtesy of Publishers Development Corporation.

"Deep Thinking From Top Social Scientists" appeared originally as "CCW Reform Movement Spreads Despite Bogus Anti-CCW 'Study'" in *American Handgunner,* September/October 1995. It is reprinted here courtesy of Publishers Development Corporation.

"Whose Life Is It, Anyway?" appeared originally as "HCI Launches Attack Against CCW Laws Without Facts, Logic" in *American Handgunner,* November/December 1997. It is reprinted here courtesy of Publishers Development Corporation.

"Utility, Destroyer of Rights" appeared originally as "Landmark Study Proves More Guns Reduce Crime" in the January/February 1999 edition of *American Handgunner,* "Benevolent Dictators Love Guns Because Gun Owners Do Great Good" in the March/April 1999 edition of *American Handgunner,* "Theory of the 'Smoking' Gun: Utilitarianism and Gun Control" in the July/August 1999 issue *American Handgunner,* and "That Carrying Concealed Guns Lowers Crime Is Not Relevant to Gun Debate" in the September/October issue of *American Handgunner.* The combined articles are reprinted here courtesy of Publishers Development Corporation.

"The Second Amendment is Dead" appeared originally as "Like An Atrophied Limb, The 2nd Amendment Has Died of Neglect" in *American Handgunner*, November/December 1995. It is reprinted here courtesy of Publishers Development Corporation.

"The Unbearable Lightness of Rights" appeared originally as "Who Protects Your Rights? You, As A Member Of A Jury" in American Handgunner, May/June 2000 and as "The Supreme Court Will Never Safeguard Your Gun Rights"in *American Handgunner*, July/August 2000. It is reprinted here, with minor modifications, courtesy of Publishers Development Corporation.

"Walter Mitty's Second Amendment" appeared originally in *American Handgunner*, September/October 1997. It is reprinted here courtesy of Publishers Development Corporation.

"The Line in the Sand" appeared originally in *American Handgunner*, March/April 1995. It is reprinted here courtesy of Publishers Development Corporation.

Quotations:

The quotation of Richard Adams at the beginning of the book is from *Watership Down,* the chapter titled, "The Shining Wire," at page 129 of the current paperback edition published by Avon Books, Inc., © Rex Collings, Ltd., 1972.

The quotation of Heraclitus at the beginning of the section, "Bearing Arms," is from *Selections from Early Greek Philosophy,* Milton C. Nahm (Prentice-Hall, Inc., 1964), page 75.

The quotation of Sir William Blackstone at the beginning of the section, "Against Prevention," is from 4 *Commentaries* 21.

The quotation of Soren Kierkegaard at the beginning of the section, "Against Utility," is from *Concluding Unscientific Postscript to Philosophical Fragments,* translated by Howard V. Hong and Edna H. Hong (Princeton University Press, 1992), Vol. 1, page 135.

The quotation of George Ripert at the beginning of the section, "Second Amendment," is from *Le Déclin du Droit. Etude sur la législation contemporaine* (Paris: Librairie Générale de Droit et de Jurisprudence, 1949), p. 94.

A Note About Rabbits

For those who are not intimately familiar with the story, *Watership Down*, the choice of a selection from a story about rabbits who are looking for a new home at the beginning of a work on gun control will likely seem incomprehensible, if not bizarre. Those who love the book will readily understand. For everyone else, I append this small explanation, with apologies to Richard Adams.

A small group of rabbits has abandoned its warren in fear of its impending destruction and is in search of a new home. After they have already traveled far and braved many dangers, they stumble upon a warren that seems like heaven on earth. For one thing, the food is abundant. A farmer dumps old vegetables nearby that the rabbits enjoy, and the farmer kills all the predators. The underground warren itself is palatial, luxurious.

But the rabbits who live there are strange. They have given up telling the old tales about the Great Rabbit, El-ahrairah. Instead, they have invented songs and have taken to reciting strange poetry and creating abstract art on the warren walls.

Amazingly, the rabbits who live there are not hostile to the rabbits who are searching for a new home, and don't seem concerned

173

with protecting their turf; they readily invite the wandering rabbits to join them. This raises some suspicions among the traveling rabbits, because this behavior is so un-rabbit-like. But virtually all of the wandering rabbits are tired of their journey, worn out by fear and just want to settle down, particularly in such inviting circumstances. Only one of them, Fiver, a seer, steadfastly opposes the move and refuses to join the warren, remaining outside, and insisting that they travel to Watership Down.

Then one morning, Bigwig, the biggest and strongest of the wandering rabbits, is caught in a snare. He is dying; he may already be dead. The wandering rabbits ask the other rabbits to come help them save their friend, but the warren rabbits become very angry and pretend nothing is happening.

It now becomes apparent what *is* happening. The farmer has cultivated the warren for his own use. He takes care to keep the rabbits well fed and kills their enemies, but is cautious enough not to harvest so many rabbits that he would scare them away. The eagerness of the other rabbits to have the wandering rabbits join their warren is also now plain. The more rabbits, the less any particular rabbit risks being snared. The warren rabbits have made a bargain with death, have given up the risks and burdens that come with freedom in exchange for protection in a kind of welfare state that does, indeed, provide comfort and security -- the greatest good -- for the greatest number. In place of the stories that served to fit them for living as free rabbits and to relish that life, they have created a new mythology of abstract art, designed to dignify, rationalize and cover up their Faustian bargain. The quotation is part of Fiver's speech after Bigwig has been rescued, and his summation of the nature of the warren.

This story, from the time I first read it, seemed to me one of the most stinging, telling critiques of modernity I have ever read. To my mind it captures perfectly the modern mindset, including that of the anti-gun movement: the renunciation of responsibility for living freely, the search for safety and welfare provided by, and at the expense of, others.